CHRONICLES OF OLD LONDON
EXPLORING ENGLAND'S HISTORIC CAPITAL

© 2012 Kevin Jackson

Published in the United States by:
Museyon, Inc.
20 E. 46th St., Ste. 1400
New York, NY 10017

Museyon is a registered trademark.
Visit us online at www.museyon.com

ISBN 978-0-9846334-3-2

1259320

Printed in China

For the Parsons family of London W12
—Henrietta, Roger, Harry and Emma—
With gratiude and love.

*L*ondoners love to complain about their town: they always have.
They will say that it's dirty, it's horribly crowded, the once-
magnificent public transport systems are now unreliable at best,
the price of everyday necessities is ridiculous and the price
of housing insane. There is truth in all of this, especially the
bit about house prices.

But London can also be one of the world's most agreeable cities
both to live in and to visit, and some of the best things about it are
still free – a stroll in one of the many parks, a visit to most of the
major museums and art galleries (admission charges were applied
for a while in the 1980s and 1990s but many of them have been
lifted), window-shopping in the West End, quiet reflection in the
magnificent City churches. And though there are some districts
you would not be wise to visit at any time of the day, central
London remains one of the safest of the world's capital cities.

All of these experiences, as well as the more expensive ones like
a trip to the theatre in Shaftesbury Avenue or a grand restaurant
in Covent Garden, will be enriched if you know something about
the histories that have shaped the place. To the informed eye,
London is almost endlessly fascinating: maybe not as exciting as
New York, as theatrically beautiful as Paris or as enchanting as
Venice, but—in my view, at least—richer in narratives than any of
those fine towns.

Here are a few of the stories which have made
London what it is today.

17th century map of London, originally started by W.Hollar, student of German engraver Mattheus Merian. Published in the Netherlands, After 1688

BLE OF CONTENTS

WALKING TOURS

PLACES REFERENCED OUTSIDE LONDON

THE UNITED KINGDOM

Buckland Monachorum: Final Home of Francis Drake; Drake's Drum

Canterbury: Assassination of Archbishop Thomas Becket; Canterbury Tales

Gads Hill Place: Country Home of Charles Dickens

Hastings: King Harold's Army Vanquished by Norman Invaider William the Conqueror in 1066

Hever Castle: Boleyn Family Home; Catherine of Aragon Banished here by Henry VIII

Oxford: Burnings of the Anglican Oxford Martyrs

Plymouth: Drake Sets out to Face the Spanish Armada

Salisbury: Clarendon Palace, Home of Henry II

Stratford-upon-Avon: Birthplace of William Shakespeare; Royal Shakespeare Company

Weymouth: First Reports of Plague in England

FRANCE

Agincourt: Henry V Defeats the French, 1415

Bayeux: Tapestry Celebrating Victories of William the Conqueror

Calais: Victory of Henry V

Honfleur: Victory of Henry V

Jumièges: Norman Church that Inspired Westminster Abbey

Meaux: Henry V Dies in Battle

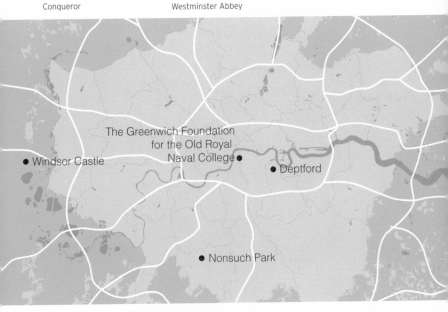

GREATER LONDON

Depford: Francis Drake Knighted Upon the Golden Hind

Nonsuch Park: Residence of Queen Elizabeth I

The Greenwich Foundation for the Old Royal Naval College: Funeral of Lord Nelson

Windsor Castle: Charles I Buried; Home of Queen Victoria

CHAPTER 1

BOUDICCA REVOLTS AGAINST THE ROMANS; LONDINIUM BURNS

60 A.D.

The area of land now occupied by London was once seabed; fossils of ancient marine life from the Upper Jurassic period can be found in the local stone. When the waters finally retreated, they left a broad, shallow valley, made up of marshes and mud flats, streams and small rivers—and one great river. The Thames, broader and shallower in its early days, ran from the heart of England to the North Sea. About 5,000 years ago, Southern English tribes began to gather in greater numbers at a particular spot on the Thames, about 40 miles inland, where the water was shallow enough to be forded with ease. They practiced trade and they learned to work iron and bronze. Merchants came from Spain and Gaul, and possibly as far away as the eastern Mediterranean. Next, Celtic tribes moved in to the growing city and gradually developed a culture of astonishing complexity and stability. A new city began to thrive, born from commerce, but cursed to suffer a thousand years of invasion, rebellion, blood and death.

London enters the written record in 54 B.C., when Julius Caesar, anxious to subdue Gaul, decided that it was time to claim "Britannia" for Rome, base a powerful army there and so secure the flanking area across the English Channel, while extending Roman hegemony further still. His armies—2,000

⟨ *Boadicea Haranguing the Britons*, by John Opie, 1793

Ancient Britons gather to fight the landing Roman fleet

cavalry and five legions, each consisting of thousands of men—landed at Deal, in what is today the county of Kent. He was met with keen resistance from an army headed by a local king, Cassivellaunus, but in the end the natives were no match for the discipline of the mighty Roman army. Caesar found the London fording point, crossed the Thames and forced the Britons to make an ignominious retreat.

It took a second Roman invasion, in 43 A.D., to fully secure Londinium for Roman rule—40,000 legionnaires tore into the native resistance forces from all sides—but only a decade or so after this massacre, the city had settled into a peaceful and increasingly prosperous way of life. The historian Tacitus wrote of it as a city famous for its *negotiators*— businessmen, traders, merchants. At its center were low structures built of the local clay: smithies, shops, taverns, stores. Some Londoners lived here, but most lived a little further back from the river, mainly in the traditional native round huts. Such idyll proved brief.

On the fringes of the Roman Empire's territory in Southern England, trouble began to brew with the Iceni, an East Anglian tribe allied with the Romans, but not under their rule. That changed when the Iceni king, Prasutagus, died around 60 A.D. To fulfill an agreement with the Roman authorities, Prasutagus left control of his territory to both his daughters and the Roman Empire. The Romans, believing that inheritance could only pass to male heirs, seized the land from Prasutagus's queen, the tall and clever Boudicca (also recorded as Boudica and Boadicea). Legionnaires flogged her and raped her daughters. Hungry for revenge, the angry queen sacked the Roman settlement at Colchester and then marched on London. Since its governor, Gaius Suetonius Paulinus, was away in the North trying to secure the borderlands, Londinium was all but defenseless.

According to Tacitus, the locals were "massacred, hanged, burned and crucified." The total death toll may have been as high as 70,000.
The vengeful Boudicca then set fire to the city, burning it to the ground. Archaeologists have discovered a thin layer of red earth spread right across the site of the fire, made up of oxidized metal, burned wood and fired clay. Coins have been found near London Bridge, melted into strange shapes by the inferno. Boudicca's fire was the first of the many that have afflicted the city and by far the worst—her arson was the only one ever to destroy the place entirely.

Returning from the North, the governor's armies put down the revolt; it is not clear whether Boudicca died of illness or after poisoning herself to avoid defeat. The Romans rebuilt Londinium swiftly, and entirely to their own tastes, constructing Roman temples, an amphitheater, a forum and rows of shops and houses laid out in formal squares after the Italian model. (Very few traces of this period remain, the most famous being the ruins of the Temple of Mithras in the City of London.) Once again, trade thrived and the population swelled. By 250 A.D. there were about 30,000 inhabitants, making Londinium by far the largest city in Britannia and the fifth largest Roman settlement north of the Alps.

All went well until the Empire began to crumble. In 286, the senior Roman commander Carausius mutinied and declared Britannia his own kingdom. Seven years later, this *coup d'état* was put down by the Emperor Constantius Chlorus, who rebuilt the city's defenses against likely attack by Germanic pirates, Picts and other enemies. But Rome's grip was weakening. When Rome itself came under attack by Alaric the Goth early in the fifth century, the Emperor Honorius told Britain that it must now fend for itself.

The period that followed, from 410 A.D. to 1066 A.D., is in large measure a bloody, confusing tale of invasions—some successfully resisted, some overpoweringly strong. At first, there was little in the way of cultural influence from these skirmishes. The first sets of invaders, the Angles and the Saxons—Germanic tribes, who came from the territories that are now Germany and the Netherlands—were semi-nomadic peasant warriors, not all that interested in settled life. Raiders from the North Sea largely killed off what was left of Roman maritime trade, and the city went into an economic decline that lasted for the better part of three centuries. Despite this period

Viking attack on Britain

of recession, the Angles and Saxons (who inevitably began to intermarry, thus producing the Anglo-Saxons; the period from about 550 to 1066 is usually called the Anglo-Saxon stage of English history) finally began to settle in London and build houses. They also built churches, since, by the start of the seventh century, Christianity had displaced the older religions. A Roman monk, Mellitus, was made Bishop of London and founded a wooden cathedral dedicated to St. Paul. By the time of the Norman Invasion in 1066, London had a hundred parishes, with one church for every three acres.

Trade slowly revived, and by the early eighth century London was once again, as a contemporary writer put it, "the mart of many nations." Britain in general and London in particular were not as highly developed as cities in France and Italy, partly because they were not yet as rich, partly because the land was in many ways provincial—not nearly so open to the innovating forces of trade from which cities on the Continent had benefitted. Still, they were starting to catch up. Above all, London grew steadily richer on the export of wool to the Continent, as it would for centuries. Once again, though, the time of peace and plenty was short-lived. From 834, Vikings began to plague England, and London was a key target for plunder and slaughter. The horrors lasted for two hundred years, and the tide only turned under the rule of King Alfred of Wessex, who reigned from 871-899. In 886, he seized the city from Viking control and turned it into a fortress. He restored the ancient walls that had been breached or simply allowed to fall into ruin, and he rebuilt the quays that had been destroyed by war. He also built a large road, just inside the city walls, which ran from Aldgate to Ludgate; a few traces of it still exist in the modern City district.

More Viking attacks were to come about a century later, but by now London was ready. A massive invasion attempt in 984 was resisted so ferociously that for once the Vikings suffered far more than the Londoners. Subsequent assaults, just as bloody, led to further short-term victories for the Vikings. In the long term, though, London prevailed. When the Danish prince Cnut

King Alfred the Great (849-899)

(Canute) was accepted by Londoners as King of All England in 1016, his crowning was as much a product of tactful diplomacy between him and his Anglo-Saxon equals as of a local surrender to Cnut's superior military forces. Under Cnut, London supplanted Winchester as the capital city of England. The center of trade was now also the national center of power, religion and culture, and it has remained so ever since.

Throughout the early eleventh century, London began to find stability after centuries of recurrent crisis. A system of parish communities grew in the city, building strong social bonds. Trade revived yet again and religious communities were founded. Londoners could feel confident that the terrors and miseries of the last centuries were finally at an end.

They were not.

THE EARLIEST LONDONERS

Thousands of years before London became the metropolis we know today, mammoths roamed the land. In 1690, excavators discovered a mammoth's remains near the site of what is now King's Cross railway station. Inside the beast was a flint axe that has been dated to the Paleolithic era. *Homo sapiens* has been hunting, eating and sleeping in these parts for at least half a million years, though the first signs of consistent occupation are only some 15,000 years old. Relics of those Mesolithic and Neolithic times, including pottery, tools, feast-pits and waste, have been found just south of the Thames in Southwark and Clapham, and to the north in Hampstead.

CHAPTER 2.

THE DEDICATION OF WESTMINSTER ABBEY
28 DECEMBER 1065

He may have been an albino. He was certainly said to be very pale; also plump, mild mannered, kindly, pious and dangerously weak. Edward of England, known also as "Edward the Confessor," has left few enduring marks. Historians have often been harsh to him, depicting him as a man too preoccupied with religious matters to care much about the good of his realm—more of a monk than a monarch. ("Confessor" signifies a man who lived a saintly life, but was never a churchman or a martyr.) In effect, he was a puppet king, set on the throne of England in April 1043 by a warrior Earl Godwin, who had been the most powerful man in the land for about 24 years. It is doubtful we would remember Edward's name at all were it not for the one great gift he left the nation: Westminster Abbey.

Edward commissioned the Abbey with the intention that it should be his burial place. He eventually had his wish. Though the building, begun sometime between 1043 and 1052, was not completed until 1090, Edward lived just long enough to hear that it had been dedicated, on December 28, 1065; "hear" rather than "see" because he was already too feeble to rise from his sick bed. He died a week later on January 5, 1066, after muttering a hair-raising prophecy of dark times ahead for the kingdom that terrified

---

‹ Left panel of the *Wilton Diptych*, c. 1395: Edmund the Martyr, Edward the Confessor and John the Baptist present Richard II to the Virgin and Child.

King Edward the Confessor sends Harold to Normandy, Bayeux Tapestry, c. 1070s

all but one of his attendants. (The unmoved listener was Archbishop Stigand, who whispered in the ear of Edward's appointed heir Harold II that the poor old man was raving mad.) Edward's remains were buried in the Abbey and are there to this day.

It is possible, however, that Edward was a much less pious and much more vigorous man than he appears in the stories the Church sponsored about him, stories that ultimately led to his being canonized in 1161 by Pope Alexander III. Edward was even the Patron Saint of England, until the adoption of St. George during the Hundred Years' War.

Through the haze of sanctity, glimpses of a decidedly un-saintly head of state sometimes emerge, as when, in 1054, he ordered an army to Scotland to attack a troublesome local warrior named Macbeth. And if Edward was motivated in part by piety to commission the Abbey, he also had good political reasons to flex his regal muscles by ordering a grand monument to his reign; abbeys and monasteries were under royal, not aristocratic, patronage.

The idea of building the Abbey—or, more exactly, of entirely rebuilding the Benedictine foundation that had already existed there—is said to have come to Edward in a dream, which seems fitting, since the ground on which it was built had long been associated with dreams and visions. A document of the eighth century calls it "that terrible place," meaning not that it was disgusting, but that it inspired sensations of holy terror. Legend tells that in the seventh century, on the night before the consecration of the Saxon church of St. Peter on the site, a humble fisherman from the south of the river in Lambeth met St. Peter himself, who asked to be rowed across the Thames. St. Peter stepped inside the new church and at once it was lit up by an intense brilliance, as though a thousand candles were burning. It was the story of St. Peter's visit that inspired the name "West" Minster—as a complement to the East Minster over in the City, devoted to St. Paul. A thousand years later, the London poet William Blake had a vision of monks walking down the central aisle of the Abbey. Perhaps he had gazed back through time and seen the community of Benedictines that was established here by St. Dunstan in 960.

North view of Westminster Abbey c. 1689, Engraving by T. Collins

When it came to the design of his monument, Edward, who had been educated by Normans, was deeply influenced by Norman culture: It was his decision that the Abbey should be built in the Norman Romanesque style, of which a major defining feature is the presence of large, semi-circular arches above windows and doors. Westminster Abbey was the first Norman Romanesque church in England; it was very similar in looks to the Abbey at Jumièges, built at roughly the same time.

Almost as soon as Edward died, the Abbey became a building of State as well as Church. Edward had been crowned king in Winchester, the capital city of Wessex, but Harold was crowned in the Abbey, as William of Normandy would be just a few months later. From that point on, the Abbey became the official place of coronations, and often of royal funerals and weddings, too. Edward's Abbey lasted until the reign of Henry III, who in 1245 ordered the church to be rebuilt in the Anglo-Gothic style. Work staggered on as late as 1517, though much of it was completed during the reign of Richard II and under the direction of the great architect Henry Yevele.

Henry III's creation is largely the building we still see today, though subsequent monarchs and architects have chipped in with afterthoughts. In 1503, Henry VII commissioned a chapel in honor of the Virgin Mary; Nicholas Hawksmoor designed two new towers, which weren't built until

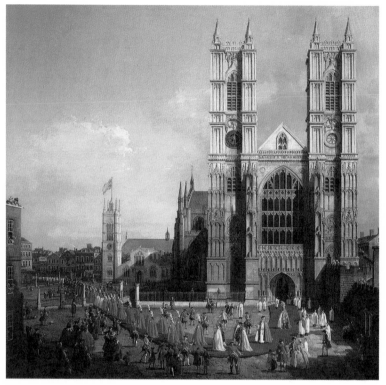

Westminster Abbey with a Procession of Knights of the Bath, by the Italian painter Canaletto, 1749

after his death. The Abbey's fortunes waxed and waned according to the political and religious turbulence of successive ages. From 1540 to 1550, Henry VIII granted it Cathedral status so as to exempt it from his own policy of looting and destroying monastic foundations. Under Mary, the Catholic queen, it was given back to the Benedictines; under Elizabeth it was immediately reclaimed for England and Protestantism.

The clerics and scholars who assembled within its walls made the Abbey the third most important center of learning in England, after Oxford and Cambridge. One of the three teams that worked on the translation of the King James Bible was based here and produced, roughly, the first third of the Old Testament and the last half of the New Testament.

Interior of Westminster Abbey. *Queen Victoria's Golden Jubilee Service, Westminster Abbey, 21 June 1887*, by William Ewart Lockhart, 1887-1890

As the Abbey grew central to the nation's ceremonial life, it became the custom to bury the great and the good under its stones—even regicide Oliver Cromwell was initially laid to rest in the Abbey, though his body was later dug up and decapitated. No doubt to the horror of some believers, Charles Darwin was buried in Westminster Abbey (April 1882), as suitable company throughout eternity for Sir Isaac Newton (March 1727), who rests nearby.

Thanks to television, and to events such as the funeral of Princess Diana in 1997, the interior of the Abbey has been witnessed by countless millions of people around the world. It has become such a potent emblem of its city that some writers have chosen to take its foundation as a point of figurative rebirth. To many Londoners, it was a source of deep comfort that—like St. Paul's Cathedral, its spiritual sibling to the east—the Abbey survived the Blitz almost unscathed. Perhaps the albino king was looking many centuries into the future when he made his dying prophecies?

CHAPTER 3

THE CORONATION OF WILLIAM THE CONQUEROR

25 DECEMBER 1066

Westminster Abbey was overflowing with English men and women of all stations, who gathered at the hallowed ground for the third major event to take place there in less than one year. First, in January, there was the funeral of Edward the Confessor. Then, almost immediately after, followed the coronation of Harold Godwinson, the new King Harold II. Now there was another coronation, this time for William, the ferocious Norman invader whose armies had killed King Harold and destroyed his forces at the coastal town of Hastings, just over fifty miles away to the southeast. Up to the very moment at which the crown was to be placed on the new king's head, most of the service had been identical to Harold's coronation. But there was one significant addition. The two presiding archbishops, Ealdred of York and Geoffrey de Mowbray of Coutances, presented the king-elect to the congregation and asked if they would have William crowned. There was a giant roar of acclamation.

This proved to be a disaster. Norman soldiers, stationed outside the church in case of an English counterattack, mistook all the shouting for a riot. They set fire to the surrounding houses and turned their swords on bystanders. The cathedral's magnificent windows glowed with flames, while full-on

---

< *Conqueror Crowned*, a depiction of the coronation of William the Conqueror by John Cross, 1754

The Battle of Hastings, 1066

panic broke out. Screaming, struggling people who feared they would burn to death fought their way out through the doors, leaving only a handful of brave souls to complete the ceremony. Those present were astonished to see that William — who, whatever his faults, was a man of deep courage — was "violently trembling." Even the bravest man is permitted to fear God, and it seemed to William that God had just shown his anger in the clearest way.

The invasion that had led to this ceremony had been unusually swift. One contemporary historian claimed that William had conquered all of England in a single day, "between the third hour and the evening." There is a grain of truth in this, though armed resistance to Norman rule continued in parts of Britain until 1071 and broke out again in later years. Military strategists have often blamed Harold II for losing England by staking everything on a single battle with William's army — a battle staged when his forces were tired to the point of exhaustion. Still, no less an authority than Winston Churchill would agree centuries later that it was reasonable for Harold to have had faith in his loyal, if brutal, axe men. After all, they had at the time just won a major victory in the north of England.

Two invasions of Britain took place in 1066; the first came from Scandinavia. In September, news reached London that a large Norwegian fleet had sailed up the Humber river and established a military base at Stamford Bridge, near the city of York. Harold swiftly set out northward along the Roman road that led from London to York, gathering recruits as he went, and fell on the Norsemen much earlier than they had expected. Both sides fought hard, until one of the two Norse commanders was killed. Harold offered a truce and pardons for all survivors, but he was refused, and battle began again. The Norwegians were slaughtered. Had William not invaded soon after, Harold would have been remembered as a triumphant warlord.

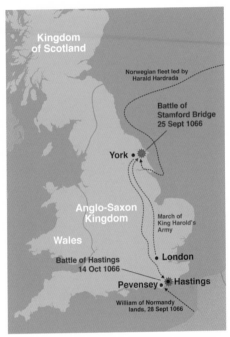

Harold's Road to Battle

But the Norman forces landed at Pevensey Bay on September 28th and were met with almost no local resistance. News reached Harold while the battle in the north was still being fought. Harold and his war-scarred forces rode back to London without a pause and covered the 200 miles in just seven days. In London, Harold rallied all the additional forces he could over the next five days, and then marched south again towards the coast. On the evening of October 13th, he took up position on the slope of a hill that stood between William's army and the path to London: Senlac Hill, about eight miles to the north of Hastings itself. At daybreak, William sent his army to attack.

It was a combat of two different military techniques. William's army was mainly cavalry, heavily reinforced by archers. Harold had foot soldiers and

The Death of Harold Godwinson at the Battle of Hastings, by James Doyle, 1864

used horses only for transport, not attack. At first, the English style seemed to prevail. Wave upon wave of William's cavalry charged against the densely ranked English, but they might as well have been attacking a mountain. The left wing of William's cavalry retreated—a desperate move that ultimately proved invaluable to his victory. Less disciplined infantrymen broke ranks to pursue the retreating horsemen and were sliced to pieces by William's elite troops. The battle tide began to turn. Harold's foot soldiers fought on with a stubbornness the Normans had never before seen. Arrows rained down on them with lethal efficiency, yet they fought on, wedged so tightly that the dead could not fall down but remained upright, shoulder-to-shoulder with the living.

Finally, in a brilliant coup, William staged a fake retreat, hoping that it would have the same effect as the genuine retreat of that morning. It worked. The less well-trained infantry raced halfway down the hill in pursuit and were cut to shreds. Finally, as night fell, only Harold and his immediate bodyguard were left to resist. William ordered his archers to

William the Conqueror

fire high, so that their arrows would fall behind the shield wall. Harold was struck and he died. (Or so the traditional story goes. Some recent historians claim he died by the sword.) Fighting continued and large numbers of Norman horsemen were killed in the following hours, but William knew he had won.

Instead of taking a direct route to London, William set about subduing resistance throughout Kent. When the people of Romney killed an out-riding band of Norman knights, he had the place massacred. Rumors of these actions spread, as a contemporary put it, "like flies settling on a wound." Intimidated villages rushed to swear loyalty to him. William's forces circled the capital, leaving terror in their path and isolating London, in Churchill's words, "by a belt of cruel desolation." London had no stomach to resist. Within two years, William's wife Matilda came from France to be crowned at Westminster; later that year, their fourth son, the future King Henry I, was born. And so, it is reasonable to say, was modern England.

For the next thousand years, every attempt to invade Britain was thwarted.

CHAPTER 4.

SAINT THOMAS BECKET ASSASSINATED IN CANTERBURY

29 DECEMBER 1170

There were four killers. Winter's early, deep shadows were already turning the cold afternoon into frigid night when they burst into Canterbury Cathedral. Their sharp sword blades glittered in the candlelight. They had been drinking heavily the night before, and their heads were shrouded with cloaks.

"Where is the traitor?" they shouted. Thomas Becket, Archbishop of Canterbury, dressed in his full ecclesiastical splendor, calmly stared them down. "Here I am. No traitor, but a priest of God. What do you want?"

He knew quite well what they wanted, and so did his attendants. All but two of Becket's men fled. The priest did not stand a chance, but he remained cool and defiant.

The hooded men came forward. Suddenly, something snapped inside Becket. As if he were once again a tough, scrappy little boy in Cheapside, he began to yell coarse insults at them: "Pimp! Pimp!" This enraged the assassins and they rushed forward for the kill. The first blow sliced off the top of Becket's skull, as neatly as you might slice a boiled egg; the crown dangled by a

< *The Martyrdom of St. Thomas*, detail from the St. Thomas Altarpiece by Meister Francke, commissioned in 1424

29

Canterbury Cathedral

single string of flesh. A second blow pierced him, then a third. He fell to his knees and cried out that he was ready to embrace death. The fourth blow was terrible: The sword sliced Becket's head in half, and its point shattered against the paving stones. The fifth blow was intended as a hideous insult to Becket's corpse. His murderer put his foot squarely on the back of Becket's neck, stuck his sword inside the skull, scooped out brains and blood and scattered them in all directions. "Let us away, knights. He will rise no more."

We owe our detailed knowledge of the atrocities that took place on December 29, 1170 to the eyewitness testimony of a brave monk with the fitting name of Edward Grim. Grim was one of the two attendants who stood by Becket during the attack and was himself wounded in the arm by the killer's first blow. He wrote his account of the murder some years later, after Becket had been canonized, so there might have been some attempt to play up the element of martyrdom. But the essential details are true.

News of Becket's murder spread with rare speed throughout England and all Christendom, and it took less than three years for Pope Alexander III to declare him a saint, in February 1173. As the news spread, it was widely accepted that the person who had ordered his murder was none other than

Becket's former close friend and patron, King Henry II.

There have been about forty native-born English saints (counting the pre-Normans as English), but only two of them are well known: St. Thomas More and St. Thomas Becket, both of whom were executed after coming into conflict with their monarch about the extent of Crown authority over the Church.

Thomas Becket occupies a special place in the story of London. He was born in the city's market district of

The martyrdom of St. Thomas Becket

Cheapside in 1118, and throughout the Middle Ages he enjoyed a significant cult following as one of the city's two patron saints—the other being St. Paul. By the early thirteenth century, Becket's image was part of the city's heraldry; early versions of the Common Seal of the City of London featured the saint, dressed in his ecclesiastical robes, seated on an arch overlooking a panorama of the City. Thanks to the success of modern dramas, including T.S. Eliot's *Murder in the Cathedral* and Jean Anouilh's *Becket*, most people know more about his death than his life. But his life has plenty of interest of its own.

According to one traditional telling, he was born on December 21, 1118—the feast day of Thomas the Apostle. His parents, Gilbert and Matilda, were both of Norman descent. Gilbert Becket was a wealthy merchant, and his personal success story was part of London's success story. By the middle of the twelfth century, the city was thriving. The banks of the Thames, north and south, were crammed with working docks, where ships were loaded with wool (England's chief export) or unloaded of their bolts of silk and vats of wine. Merchants and workers swarmed around in large numbers— there were almost 25,000 Londoners by now—and, day and night, the

King Henry II

air was filled with the smells of roasting meat and fish from the bankside cookshops.

Gilbert first grew rich on trading, and then he became richer as a construction boss. He enjoyed his wealth to the fullest, building one of the grandest houses in Cheapside, 100 feet deep and with a 40-foot frontage. In the normal course of things, Thomas might well have followed in his father's footsteps. But he was a bright child and he did what many intelligent lads were doing: He sought a career in the church. After studies at a local grammar school and in Paris, he managed to find suitable clerical posts and eventually joined the household of Theobald, Archbishop of Canterbury.

This career choice was hardly any indication of piety. The Church was an excellent route to power and status for sons of common folk, and men of the cloth could also be influential men of state. By his late twenties, Thomas had attained the rank of Archdeacon, and his accomplishments drew the attention of King Henry II. In January 1155, Henry made Thomas his Lord Chancellor, and Thomas became a vigorous enforcer of the King's traditional right to draw revenues from many sources, including the church. They became close, and Henry even sent his son to live as part of Becket's household. The boy later said that he had experienced more paternal love from Thomas than he had ever known from his royal father.

But this chummy relationship began to sour after May of 1162, when Becket was appointed Archbishop of Canterbury. Once very much the king's man, he now began to take his vocation seriously. He prayed earnestly, renounced earthly comforts and began to wear a penitential hair shirt under his rich vestments, so that his skin was perpetually itchy. And, inevitably, he began to take the care of his Church more seriously. This did not please Henry, who was planning to extend his power still further. At the end of January 1164, Henry summoned his bishops to Clarendon Palace and demanded that they sign a resolution that would weaken the English Church's links with Rome and minimize its independence from royal control. Only Thomas refused.

The conflict between Thomas and Henry deepened, to the point where Thomas had to flee to France, where Louis VII offered him protection. Thomas took refuge in a Cistercian monastery, until Henry threatened the order with reprisals. Matters came to a head in June 1170, when Henry—following a strange but not unprecedented protocol—decided to have his fifteen-year-old son (known as Henry the Young King) crowned at York.

Thomas retaliated by excommunicating both Henry and the three bishops who had taken part in the ceremony. It was then that the quick-tempered Henry exploded, shouting "What miserable drones and traitors have I nourished and brought up in my household who allow their lord to be treated with such shameful contempt by a low-born cleric?" Four of the knights in his company chose to treat this angry outburst as Becket's death warrant. They saddled their horses and set off for Canterbury.

CHAPTER 5.

THE CORONATION OF RICHARD I AT WESTMINSTER
3 SEPTEMBER 1189

Richard I was a strikingly handsome man: well over six feet tall, with piercing blue eyes and flowing red-gold hair inherited from his mother, Eleanor of Aquitaine. Richard was much more like her than his father, Henry II—he also cared more for her Continental possessions than he did for England. Richard also knew how to put on a good show. His coronation at Westminster—the first coronation for which we have a detailed record—was astonishingly lavish. Gold glittered everywhere. Attendant barons dressed the new king's ankles with golden spurs, presented him with a golden sword and held a golden canopy over his head. Richard had orchestrated the whole ceremony himself and paid careful attention to its political symbolism. Following an example set by the Holy Roman Emperor Charlemagne, Richard himself picked up the crown and handed it over to Baldwin of Forde, the Archbishop of Canterbury, who was then to place it on Richard's brow. The message could hardly have been more clear: the King first, the Church second.

It was an awe-inspiring performance and it went off almost perfectly, save for one small omen—a bat, flittering about Richard's throne in broad daylight. Such portents were taken seriously by many members of the

Richard I the Lionheart, King of England, by Merry-Joseph Blondel, 1841

congregation. Maybe they were right to be worried, for things quickly turned ugly. Richard had issued an instruction that there should be no women and no Jews at the ceremony. Despite this, a number of prominent Jewish men arrived bearing gifts for their new monarch. Richard's courtiers pounced on them, stripped them naked and had them flogged.

Distorted word of this filtered out to the common people of London, who gathered that the new King had ordered that all Jews be murdered. Mob violence erupted: Prominent Jews were beaten, robbed, forcibly converted to Christianity or burned alive. This went on for two days. In a written chronicle, the monk Richard of Devizes referred to it as a *holocaustum*; this was the first recorded use of such a term.

Richard could be a savage warrior, but he saw no sense in these bigoted civilian murders and issued a royal writ demanding that the Jews be left alone and that the worst of the rioters should be executed. (Sadly, the massacres of Jews began again as soon as Richard went off to the Crusades.)

Yet there is something grimly warranted about the violence surrounding Richard's coronation, since his life was largely devoted to waging war—not only against the Moors, but also against his father, his brother and his former allies. In a famous phrase British historian Steven Runciman declared Richard the Lionheart "a bad son, a bad husband and a bad king, but a gallant and splendid soldier."

Though he was born in Oxford, on September 8, 1157, and spent part of his childhood in England, Richard—raised by his mother to speak French and the southern French *langue d'Oc*—never learned English and did not greatly care for the country. He complained that it was always raining. In the ten years of his reign, he spent barely six months in England and was entirely absent in the last five years.

Battle between Richard I and Saladin in Palestine, by Philip James de Loutherbourg, c. 1791-2

Richard was the third legitimate son of Henry II—himself the great-grandson of William the Conqueror. He was only sixteen when, egged on by his mother Eleanor, he staged an armed revolt against his father. It failed and his father forgave him, but the King sent Eleanor to prison (where she remained until Henry's death). Henry then sent Richard on a military expedition to punish the same French aristocrats who had joined the rebellion. It was during this turncoat exercise that he earned the epithet *Coeur de Lion*: Lionheart. No one has ever questioned his physical courage.

The following years were politically complex and dominated by growing tension between Richard and his father. Richard's two older brothers were both dead by now, and he was next in line for the throne of England. He began to form strategic alliances, especially with Philip II of France, and once again went to war against his father's armies in that country. On July 4, 1189, a force led by Richard and Philip defeated Henry's army at Ballans; two days later, Henry II died in Chinon. Richard inherited his father's Dukedom before the month was over and he was crowned shortly

King Richard I watches Muslim prisoners being beheaded after the capture of Acre in 1189

after his return to England. By this time, Richard had "taken the cross"—vowed to join in the Crusades—and sworn an oath to renounce his former wickedness. He set off on the Third Crusade just months after being crowned, bearing a sword that had recently been dug up at Glastonbury and was believed to be King Arthur's Excalibur.

Foreign wars cost a lot of money, and Richard raised funds by every means necessary: big tax hikes and the sale of titles and land to anyone interested. He is believed to even have said, "I would have sold London if I could find a buyer!" By the summer of 1190 he had raised enough money to outfit an army of 8,000 men and a fleet of 100 ships and he set off for the Holy Land, conquering Cyprus and Sicily en route. At his mother's behest, he also agreed to marry the noblewoman Berengaria of Navarre. His forces landed at the occupied port of Acre on June 8, 1191, laid siege to the town and drove out Sultan Saladin's forces. Richard kept 2,700 Muslim hostages but later had them executed with ruthless pragmatism when he decided to push onwards.

He waged a bloody, often strategically brilliant war until both he and Saladin, the sultan of Egypt and Syria, realized they were in a stalemate and negotiated a three-year truce on September 2, 1192. Richard returned to Europe, but not to peace: He was kidnapped and imprisoned by Leopold V, Duke of Austria, and held for ransom for the suspected murder of the Duke's cousin. How much was a king's ransom? Enormous: 34 tons of gold—three times the annual revenue of the Crown. It was paid – a portion of the money became the foundation for the mint in Vienna—but the debt depressed England's economy for years to come. The final stage of Richard's life was largely spent fighting wars in France, where he died near Limoges, from a wound from a crossbow bolt, on April 6, 1199. The motto he adopted during these final campaigns remains that of the British Monarchy to the present day: *Dieu et Mon Droit*. God and my Right.

LONDON BRIDGE

Like the nursery rhyme suggests, London Bridge has fallen down or been burned down a number of times. Soon after their arrival in London, the Romans built a wooden bridge across the River Thames. That version was destroyed by Boudicca's army in 60 A.D. Roman workmen soon rebuilt it, though their works fell into neglect after

An engraving of Old London Bridge by Claes Van Visscher. The spiked heads of executed criminals can be seen above the Southwark gatehouse.

the collapse of the Empire. Later versions of the bridge, all wooden, rose and fell during the Dark Ages. A Viking attack in 1014 ended with the entire structure being dragged down into the Thames. A freak tornado in 1091 destroyed its replacement.

By the end of the eleventh century, it was decided to construct a bridge of more durable material, a proposal that had as much to do with religion as trade. A cult of Thomas Becket had reached such proportions that every pious English person wanted to make a pilgrimage to the place of his martyrdom in Canterbury, starting from a chapel on the Bridge. Work on the stone bridge lasted for 33 years, and it was finally opened under the reign of King John in 1209.

For three-and-a-half centuries after the final stone was laid in 1209, the most macabre sight in town was the Southern Gate of London Bridge. The place was festooned with iron pikes, and the point of every weapon was mounted with a human head—sometimes boiled to a clean skull, sometimes crowned with an ironic wreath of ivy, but usually just thickly coated with tar, so that the ravens and other carrion fowl would not peck away the flesh too quickly. First in the gory line of traitors was William Wallace, now more commonly known as "Braveheart," who was decapitated and spiked in 1305. Under the Tudors, Sir Thomas More was spiked in 1535, as was Thomas Cromwell in 1540. In fact, a bouquet of treacherous heads continued to greet everyone who crossed the Bridge until Charles II finally put an end to this gruesome entry to the City.

CHAPTER 6.

THE BLACK DEATH REACHES LONDON; ORIGINS OF THE PEASANTS' REVOLT
SEPTEMBER 1348–JUNE 1381

"Sweat, excrement, spittle, breath, so fetid as to be overpowering," ran a contemporary account by a French scientist of the symptoms of the Black Death. Yet even this horrifying description was incomplete, as it failed to mention the most terrifying effect of the plague: "buboes," ugly swellings of the flesh that varied in size from a small egg to a large apple. It was an agonizing disease, with no known cure, that arrived in Europe via trade routes from the East, probably originating in China. Wandering merchants left a trail of waste along the Silk Road; marmots and other small mammals fed on that waste, and disease-carrying fleas fed on the mammals. The deadly wave seems to have reached England from Gascony. A first case was reported in the coastal town that is now called Weymouth, around June 20, 1348. Three months later, Londoners began to fall sick.

The Plague thrived in densely populated cities, and London was easily England's largest, with an estimated 70,000 inhabitants. Its streets were essentially open sewers, thick with excrement and waste, while all but the richest people were crammed into small, dirty buildings with poor ventilation. It was a paradise for rats, whose coats were alive with plague-bearing fleas. Within 18 months, at least half its citizens were dead.

Those who watched spouses or children thrashing in their death agonies had almost certain knowledge that they would go the same way in just a few days. Within weeks, graveyards were full, and families dug holes in waste ground to bury loved ones. More often, whole families would die at the same time, leaving no able bodied survivor to bury them. By the early months of 1349, it was obvious that people were dying too quickly for individual burial. So Londoners formed crews and carved out great pits for the bodies in Smithfield and elsewhere. Every day they threw 100 or more corpses onto their rotting neighbors. There was little point trying to flee the city, since the plague was now spreading throughout England.

Some of the effects of the plague were unexpected and, for the fortunate survivors, not entirely bad. With laborers dying by the day, survivors could suddenly demand higher wages, and men who had previously scraped together mere subsistence suddenly found themselves prosperous and in constant employment. As entire families were wiped out, distant relatives came into unexpected inheritances and found themselves rich overnight. Lured by stories of handsome pickings, enterprising paupers from the rest of England decided to risk the plague and try to make it in the big city, where a year's residence was enough to make you a free man.

The worst of this early pandemic was over by 1350, two years after it began; it is possible that as many as 50,000 Londoners perished in a matter of 18 months. But it was very far from the end of the deadly visitation. Plague broke out again with exceptional virulence in 1361-62, and then at intervals across the next three centuries. It hit Shakespeare's London badly in 1589, returned in 1603 and then made a resurgence—its last outbreak in England—in 1665, the year of the Great Plague. The tale that it was the Great Fire of London in 1666 that finally purged the city of disease-carrying rats is almost certainly not true, but subsequent outbreaks were relatively mild and ended for good in the 19th century.

Long-term consequences of the Black Death were profound. England may have lost as much as 60 percent of its people within two years, and whole communities were wiped out; exact figures are impossible to establish. Across the known world, the population dropped from an estimated 450 million at the start of the fourteenth century to 360 million by its end. To the religious-minded, the Plague seemed like an angry visitation from God.

A priest blesses monks disfigured by the plague, from the manuscript *Omne Bonum*, by James le Palmer, 1360-1375

When it was noted that monks, nuns and priests were dying in enormous numbers, people began to question just how holy their clerics really were. In one respect, England came through the ordeal better than most nations: Thanks to firm, calm government, public order was maintained. There were no outbreaks of religious fanaticism such as were seen in France, no pogroms against minority groups. England had already expelled the Jews, so London saw none of the finger-pointing and mass executions of Jewish people that spread throughout Europe.

Another unpredictable consequence was the rise of English as a *lingua franca* across the land; previously, the ruling classes had conducted their affairs in French. As the Cornish writer John of Trevisa noted in 1385, older generations of teachers and officials were wiped out and gave way to successors who did not speak French or preferred to use English. And most historians agree that the long-term effect of the Black Death was to weaken the bonds of feudalism. It is usually seen as a major catalyst for the Peasants' Revolt of 1381—a misleading name, since many of those who took part were not peasants at all, but newly wealthy craftsmen, tradesmen and even clergy. Enraged by the demands that the new generation of laborers were making for higher wages, the landed classes had begun a policy of repression, including, in 1380, a poll tax to help finance the war against France. The aspect of the poll tax that most outraged the rebels was that it was levied equally on the rich and poor alike: three groats a household (the equivalent of a shilling, or twelve pence). A wealthy merchant would hardly notice the loss; a peasant would go hungry.

In response to this imposition, rebellions broke out all over the country. The uprising was at its most violent in London, where apprentices and others used the cover of the protests to slaughter hundreds of Flemish immigrants.

The end of the 1381 peasants' revolt and the death of of Wat Tyler at the hands of London's mayor, Walworth. King Richard II is shown both watching the killing and addressing to the peasants, c. 1385-1400

Of these slaughters, the nineteenth-century British historian George Macaulay Trevelyan wrote, "The cries of the slayers and the slain went on long after sunset, making night hideous." There were three main leaders of the Revolt: John Ball, Robert Cave and, above all, Wat Tyler. Left-wing historians like to celebrate Tyler as an early English revolutionary, and it is true that he did hold some egalitarian views. In other ways, though, he was quite reactionary. Tyler and many of his followers believed that England was being ruled in a tyrannous way by the houses of Lancaster, York and Gloucester (who were acting as a caretaking regime for the then fourteen-year-old Richard II) and believed their grievances would be met only if the King kicked out these Lords and assumed full regal power.

Gathering a rough army that, according to a contemporary historian, may have numbered as many as 50,000 men, Tyler marched through Kent, seized Canterbury, entered south London, crossed London Bridge and took the

Tower, where he beheaded Simon Sudbury, the Archbishop of Canterbury. Soon after, he camped out with his men on Clerkenwell Green, while the local Priory was put to the torch and the Prior himself, a tax collector, was also beheaded. By nightfall, it seemed as if all Clerkenwell was ablaze.

A personal appearance by Richard II saved London from further blazes. He agreed to parley with Tyler man-to-man. The result astonished almost everyone. Tyler demanded that Richard should abolish serfdom and confiscate the wealth of the church and hand it over to the people, as well as declaring the full equality of all men under the King. Richard seemingly agreed. A silence fell for long moments and was broken by Tyler calling for a flagon of ale, which he drained off in triumph. This arrogant gesture was too much for Richard's entourage. One of them shouted that Tyler was a thief and Tyler turned on him with a dagger. A bloody swordfight erupted, and Tyler was soon hacked to pieces. This could easily have set off a terrible riot, but Richard saved the day by shouting, "You shall have no captain but me!"—an ambiguous claim, but one which the mob chose to understand as Richard's declaration that he would take over from Tyler as their champion. The mob dispersed peacefully, unaware that some savage reprisals would take place over the next few weeks.

The Revolt was over, for now. But even the charismatic young king could not halt the changes that had been set in motion by national disaster. The Black Death was soon to be followed by the death of Feudal England.

DICK WHITTINGTON

The opportunities that rose from plague-decimated city gave rise to the legend of Dick Whittington, the poor country lad who became Lord Mayor of London after journeying to the city where, he hears, the streets were paved with gold. Many British people believe that Dick Whittington is an entirely fictitious character, mainly because of the popular pantomime *Dick Whittington and His Cat*, traditional Christmastime entertainment since the nineteenth century. But there really was a Richard Whittington (c. 1354-1423), a successful merchant, member of Parliament and four times Lord Mayor of London. Quite how a cat became part of the legend is uncertain—Whittington's real-life success story was probably mixed up with some older folk tale.

CHAPTER 7

GEOFFREY CHAUCER IS APPOINTED COMPTROLLER OF THE PORT OF LONDON

8 JUNE 1374

In Geoffrey Chaucer's long, yet incomplete narrative poem *The Canterbury Tales*, a motley crowd of pilgrims passes the time during their slow ride from London to Canterbury by telling stories—some pious, some chivalric, some comic and at least one deliciously filthy. It's this immense versatility that makes Chaucer such a pleasure to read, even after six centuries, but he has other virtues, as well. He was humane and compassionate in a period that could be appallingly brutal. His poetry is full of delight in the beauties and pleasures of life at a time when it was deemed proper to feel *contemptus mundi*: disgust at the world. He hated the tyranny of men over women and the arrogance of power, as well as swindlers, hypocrites and the self-righteous. And he was famous in his own time.

Born in 1340, Chaucer was a Londoner through and through; his father was a leading vintner, wealthy though not noble. Despite his low birth, Chaucer's intelligence, charm and hard work soon brought him into aristocratic, and then royal, circles; at the age of sixteen, he was taken on as a page—more like a household supervisor than a mere servant—by Elizabeth de Burgh, Countess of Ulster. The position may have allowed him time to study law at the Inns of Court; his poetry shows a detailed knowledge of legal terms—

Edward, the Black Prince of England

as well as astronomy, philosophy, classical literature and much else. Like John Milton after him, Chaucer believed that a true poet needed a formidably well-stocked mind.

Chaucer's service to the Countess brought him into contact with the royal court. When England launched its massive invasion against France on October 28, 1359—a force of almost 100,000 men—Chaucer was with them as a soldier, wearing an iron vest and helmet and showing at his collars the livery of his latest patron, Prince Lionel. Chaucer rode in the wing of the army commanded by Edward, the Black Prince.

Before long, the army was growing dangerously short of provisions, and men were sent out on foraging expeditions. On one of these sorties, during the Siege of Rheims in 1360, Chaucer was ambushed by a French squad, imprisoned and held to ransom. King Edward III paid the handsome sum of sixteen pounds to set him free—a sign that the young man was already becoming highly favored by the king and his court.

Chaucer officially joined the court in June 1367, in a position variously described as "valet" or "esquire." In the meantime, he had married his French wife, Philippa, herself a lady-in-waiting to Edward's Queen. Though Chaucer often wrote of the "woe in marriage," his own marriage was largely a happy one. He and Philippa had four children, and their son Thomas would later become distinguished in his own right as Speaker of the House of Commons.

Chaucer continued to impress in his sevice to the court. Admiring his skill as a speaker and negotiator, Edward used Chaucer as an envoy and sent him on a number of diplomatic missions, including assignments to Milan in 1368, and to Genoa and Florence in 1373. While in Italy, he met Italian writers and thinkers and read widely in Italian literature; in his later writing, Chaucer

Portrait of Geoffrey Chaucer in a detail of an initial from an illuminated manuscript of *The Canterbury Tales*, c. 1413-22

shows his awareness of Dante, Petrarch and Giovanni Boccaccio, authors working in a vernacular style unknown in England at that time.

On St. George's Day (April 23) 1374, King Edward granted Chaucer the gift of a gallon of good wine daily, possibly in acknowledgement for some of his early literary efforts, as this was the day to honor artists. (Edward's successor, Richard II, also liked Chaucer both as a man and as a writer and continued the grant until 1394, when he converted it into a pension of thirty pounds a year, a patronage that made Chaucer a forerunner of the Poets

Laureate.) Just a few weeks later, on June 8, 1374, Chaucer was appointed Comptroller of Customs for the Port of London—an important, highly coveted post that brought many perks, including a large, handsome apartment on Aldgate. He was a made man.

Geoffrey Chaucer

Chaucer's principal task as Comptroller was, essentially, to make sure that the Crown received its share of the import duties owed by all the guilds who were importing and exporting from the wharves along the Thames—accountancy work, combined with detective work, and involving hour after hour of poring over columns of figures to make sure that there was no fraud. (There usually was.) It could be exhausting work, but it varied in intensity and Chaucer could sometimes take whole days off to enjoy his family and settle to steady writing. During the twelve years he kept the office, he composed all his major works, including the first of his *Canterbury Tales*.

English literature had never seen anything like the works Chaucer produced after he returned from his Italian sojourns: The multifaceted *Canterbury Tales*, which introduced the vernacular to literature, and his epic poem about the Trojan War, *Troilus and Criseyde*, which is by turns intensely lyrical and coarsely funny, were astonishing feats of literary construction. These two poems are merely the twin peaks of a large and wonderful body of work, including the *Book of the Duchess*, the *House of Fame*, the *Legend of Good Women* and the *Parliament of Fowls*. English literature was no longer the parochial art of a small, offshore island. It had entered the European mainstream.

His writing shows an exacting and brilliant craftsman, one who revised his verses again and again until they felt perfect. His outstanding gifts were immediately recognized. His fame exceeded that of all his contemporary rivals—William Langland, John Gower, and the so-called Gawain-Poet. This was a culture that took its poets seriously, and Chaucer was amply rewarded, both with prizes and with important public offices. Hard as he worked on his poetry, Chaucer worked harder still as a diplomat, accountant and clerk of works. In the *House of Fame*, one of the poems in which he draws a comic, self-deprecating portrait of his working life, he is seen staggering home from a hard day at his office, only to sit down with his own books to study and write until he is stupefied. "Thou goost hom to thy hous anoon/ And, also dumb as any stoon,/ Thou sittest at another book/Tyl fully dawsed ys thy look."

When not in London, Chaucer spent long periods in the more rural surroundings of Kent and, in 1386, became a Member of Parliament for that county. He finally retired as Comptroller in 1389, only to take up an equally demanding post as Clerk of the King's Works, overlooking repairs to Westminster Palace and the construction of a wharf for the Tower of London. The following year, on June 22, 1390, he was made the Deputy Forester for a royal estate in the western county of Somerset—an even more demanding job.

Chaucer had good reason to fear for his future after his friend and patron Richard II was overthrown by Bolingbroke, but to his surprise, the new king chose to overlook the poet's loyal service to the deposed monarch and continued to favor him. On December 24, 1399, Chaucer took out a lease on his final home—some apartments near Westminster Abbey. He died less than a year later, on October 25, 1400, and was buried in the Abbey.

In 1556, Geoffrey Chaucer's remains were transferred to a large decorative tomb, establishing the part of the Abbey now known as Poets' Corner.

CHAPTER 8.

THE TRIUMPH OF HENRY V
23 NOVEMBER 1415

It was the grandest, most astonishing spectacle the city had ever seen. When the 29-year-old Henry V rode into London at the head of his troops, freshly back from his unexpected and dazzling triumph over the French at Agincourt, he was greeted by a vision of Heaven on Earth. As he made his way over London Bridge, he saw that it was swarming with "innumerable boys representing the angelic host, arrayed in white, with glittering wings, and their hair set with sprigs of laurel." Older Londoners were dressed as prophets and apostles, and they shouted "*Hosanna! Hosanna!*" as their monarch passed them by. Henry progressed towards Cornhill, which for the day had been converted into a giant pavilion made of rich crimson cloth. As he came closer, servants released "a great quantity of sparrows and other small birds," which soared up into the clear winter sky. But Henry himself was dressed modestly, and he refused to allow his entourage to show off his "bruised helmet and bended sword" ... "lest they [the crowd] should forget that the glory was due to God alone."

At Cheapside, a host of young maidens dressed entirely in white danced merrily around him, and "from cups in their hands blew forth golden leaves on the king." A huge throne had been placed to greet him, with an image

‹ *King Henry V*, by an unknown artist, c. late 16th or early 17th century, collection of the National Portrait Gallery, London

53

Battle of Agincourt, 15th-century miniature

of the sun, "which glittered above all things," on it; "round it were angels singing and playing all kinds of musical instruments." The crowds howled with joy and patriotic fervor, and the elite nodded their approval. Henry's victory over a French force many times the size of his relatively small and dysentery-ridden army was proof of his brilliance as a military leader. To his subjects, it proved other truths: that England was now a mighty land, and that God wanted things that way.

For the next seven years of his short reign, Henry was the head of a remarkably united and peaceful nation. He was also, after a treaty made with the French, recognized as the regent of France and heir apparent to the throne. To cement the agreement, he had married King Charles VI of France's daughter, Catherine of Valois.

The military coup was also a vindication of Henry's personal self-confidence. He had come to the throne two years earlier at the age of 27, at a time when the country had suffered years of division, feud, plots and armed conflict—the long, sour legacy of the usurpation of Richard II's throne by young Henry's father, Henry IV of the house of Lancaster.

The tale of those dark times was later made into sublime drama by Shakespeare in *Richard II*, and the two parts of *Henry IV* and *Henry V*. As a very young man, Henry was said to have been something of a hell-raiser and skirt-chaser, "fired with the torches of Venus herself"—very much like the "Prince Hal" in the first of the *Henry* plays. If so, he cast of his idleness early and set vigorously and skillfully about uniting his

The Wooing of Henry V, engraved by W. Greatbach, after a painting by W. F. Yeames, 1876

nation. His greatest gift may have been the talent of making everyone in his circle, including those who might otherwise have plotted against him, feel honored and valued. And even before his grand victory, he was able to coax from an admiring Parliament sums of money far greater than those raised by the poll tax that had sparked the Peasants' Revolt.

Despite his youth, he also had precious abilities as a martial leader, including a keen sense of military strategy and boundless determination. On the dark side, he was priggish, mindlessly convinced of Divine approval and, in war, merciless. At one point in the battle of Agincourt, wrongly believing himself to be surrounded on all sides, he had ordered a massacre of all but the most illustrious French prisoners—aristocrats, mostly, who had surrendered readily in the hope of easy ransom. As Winston Churchill wrote, accurately if quaintly: "Thus perished the flower of the French nobility."

Soon after his coronation on April 9, 1413, Henry had claimed his right to the French throne on ancestral grounds—he was a direct descendant of Edward III, King of England and France. The regnant King of France, Charles VI, was a relatively feeble character—a chronic invalid, and often not entirely right in the head. Henry's ultimate plan was to take over France and then lead both France and England in a mission to reclaim Jerusalem from the infidel—in short, to launch a new Crusade.

The French, aware of their relative military weakness, offered major concessions to Henry, including a large part of Aquitaine. But Henry was

Prince Hal and Falstaff in Shakespeare's *Henry IV*

rude and stubborn with the French ambassadors and steadily built up his army for invasion. Eventually he set off for France in August 1415, with an army that numbered about 12,000, including 7,000 archers in a fleet of 1,500 ships.

Upon landing in France, Henry's forces at once laid siege to the major port of Honfleur, taking it within five weeks; in the meantime, though, many of his troops had come down with dysentery. The French were convinced that his forces were now so weakened that they could easily be taken out, so when Henry marched on towards Calais, they blocked him with a huge army. On paper, the English forces were doomed—ill, malnourished, outnumbered by a ratio of what may have been as much as five to one. On the field, they were a disciplined, well-trained and spirited army facing an enemy that was poorly trained and ill-led. The battle of Agincourt took place on Friday, October 25, 1415: St. Crispin's Day.

Helped by the local conditions—it had rained heavily the night before, and many of the French troops were literally stuck in the mud—the English army soon defeated the French; in fact, they more or less destroyed them. A decisive factor had been the English and Welsh archers, experts in the use of the longbow. (It is still widely believed in Britain that the rude gesture of raising two fingers in an upward motion dates from this battle: The French were known, or believed, to cut those two fingers off captured longbow-men. The English waggled those fingers to show the enemy they were still dangerous.) No more than 450 or so English soldiers died; the French lost about 7,000. It was an overwhelming victory, and it broke France's will to resist. Henry knew that he could not soon fight another battle on this scale with an exhausted, dehydrated and battle-weary army, and so he set off for home.

It would be another two years after his London procession that Henry once again set sail for France, where the first part of his master plan was realized: In 1420, a treaty confirmed him as regent of the country and heir to the French throne. According to this treaty, he would take over as King when Charles VI died. But not all of France recognized the legitimacy of Henry's claim and battles continued for the rest of his life. Henry died of dysentery, during the course of a siege at Meaux in August 1422. The Crown of England passed to his son Henry VI, who was just nine months old.

After his death, Henry V became a legend almost at once; there were ballads and folk plays about the great, lost leader. But the legends told only part of the story. As the historian A. R. Myers put it: "The dark days through which England was to pass [after Henry V's death] made men mourn him as the ideal warrior-king, cut off at the height of his success and in the flower of manhood. In reality, he was fortunate in the hour of his death, for he reaped the renown from his policy of war but not the inevitable bitter harvest from it."

That was not Henry's only stroke of luck. He was also fortunate in that, almost two centuries after his death, William Shakespeare wrote *Henry V*, a drama that made him into an immortal hero, a great warrior and a great orator whose rallying cry, "Once more unto the breach!" has been quoted again and again at times of national emergency for England. Winston Churchill awarded him the highest praise: "He was more deeply loved by his subjects of all classes than any king has been in England."

CHAPTER 9

THE EXECUTION OF ANNE BOLEYN

THE TOWER OF LONDON, 19 MAY 1536

With her head tucked underneath her arm,
She walks the Bloody Tower
With her head tucked underneath her arm
At the midnight hour…

Thus are the words of a comical if macabre song written in the 1930s and still well known to many Londoners. "She" is Anne Boleyn, and the reason for her restless, headless ghost to be walking so many centuries after her death is, they will tell you, because a tyrant king, Henry VIII, killed her. Anne's ghost is so restless, apparently, that sightings place her phantasm in other locations outside London. But it is the place of her beheading, the Tower of London, that she seems most fond of patrolling by night. The best documented sighting of her ghost came in 1864, when a Major-General James Durham Dundas of the 60th Rifle Regiment looked down from a high window in the Tower and saw one of the night guards challenge a luminous white form, ready his bayonet, charge and pass right through it. The guard then fainted. Only the sworn testimony of an officer and a gentleman like the Major-General (then Captain) saved that poor guard from being found guilty of falling asleep while on watch.

‹ *Henry VIII and Anne Boleyn Deer Shooting in Windsor Forest*, by William Powell Frith, 1872   59

Anne Boleyn, c. 1533, and *King Henry VIII of England*, c. 1540, by Hans Holbein the Younger

Though Anne was Queen of England for just three years, she is almost as well known to the general public as long-serving monarchs such as Victoria or the two Elizabeths, largely because of the countless novels, plays, films and even operas that she has inspired. She had been crowned Queen Consort at Westminster Abbey on June 1, 1533. It is not clear how old she was; the best guess is that she was born sometime between 1501 and 1507, which would put her between twenty-six and thirty-two.

Anne, born into a newly wealthy family from Kent, had first joined the royal court as lady-in-waiting to Henry's first wife, Queen Catherine. At about nineteen, she was no more than averagely good-looking; the Venetian ambassador commented disparagingly that her breasts were "not much risen." But what she lacked in curves she more than made up for in seductive wiles, and men went crazy for her. The first to be smitten was a young nobleman, Henry Percy, heir to the huge Northumberland estate. The young lovers actually managed to get engaged, but Cardinal Wolsey stepped in to scold and dissuade Percy — spurred on by either King Henry or Percy's own father; the details are contentious. Percy was ordered to take a more acceptable bride, and Anne was banished to the French court for a few years.

When she returned, she rapidly won the heart of the poet and courtier Thomas Wyatt; Wyatt was married, and he admitted to her that all she could ever be to him was a mistress. Besides, Wyatt could see that the roving eye of Henry VIII, whom he called "Caesar," was now swivelling in Anne's direction. It was in the summer of 1526 that Henry's infatuation first became obvious to all the court. It was not just her overt sex appeal that drew him to Anne, but her promise of fertility. Henry was desperate for a male heir and he had come to believe that his marriage to Catherine of Aragon had been

Coronation procession of Anne Boleyn, from the book *Old and New London*, 1878

cursed, since Leviticus stated that any man who married his late brother's wife would be condemned to childlessness.

Henry's pursuit grew more intense. He showered her with gifts of jewels and pet animals and, despite his aversion to writing, penned her no fewer than seventeen ardent love letters. He banished Catherine to Hever Castle, where she fell dangerously ill from a fever, and began the tricky and complex business of having their marriage annulled. Meanwhile, Anne began to ply him with new, revolutionary books by William Tyndale and others—books that argued that an English king should not have to follow the orders of a pope. As head of a new "Church of England," Henry could legally declare himself single again. Henry liked what he read.

The time was ripe for Anne to yield. She was already pregnant when they married on January 25, 1533, and she gave birth to Elizabeth, later to be Queen Elizabeth I, on September 7th of that year. When the news reached Pope Clement VII, he was enraged and ordered Henry to return to Catherine at once. When Henry failed to comply, the Pope excommunicated him. In response, Henry introduced a Succession Act, which demanded that his subjects should swear an oath recognizing Anne as legitimate queen and denying all papal authority in England.

The Execution of Anne Boleyn, Consort to Henry VIII and Mother of Elizabeth I, by Jan Luyken, c. 1664-1712

Among the men of principle who refused to comply was Sir Thomas More, who was sent to the Tower and executed for treason on July 6, 1535.

The early months of Anne's short tenure as queen were relatively peaceful and promising. She settled into Greenwich Palace on the south side of the Thames and spent freely on her court. All was well until her firstborn proved not to be the boy doctors and astrologers had predicted. Then, around Christmas 1834, she miscarried; the fetus was found to be male. Henry began to have doubts about her capacity to produce a son. By October 1835, Anne was pregnant once more, only to miscarry again in the new year of 1836. And by this time, forces were amassing against her: Too many people sympathized with Catherine's family; too many hated the upstart Boleyns. Worse, Henry now persuaded himself that his second marriage was the work of the Devil—whether or not he truly believed it, he claimed Anne used witchcraft to make him fall for her.

Before long, highly implausible allegations of her adulteries were coming thick and fast. Thomas Cromwell orchestrated the campaign. A Flemish musician in Anne's court, Mark Smeaton, "confessed" (after being tortured) to having been her lover. The same charges were also brought against Sir Henry Norris, Sir Thomas Wyatt, Sir Richard Page and others, including her own brother George Boleyn, which, in the eyes of her accusers, made her guilty of incest as well as high treason. Only two of the men were acquitted; the rest were killed. Two days later, it was Anne's turn.

According to all contemporary accounts, Boleyn made as dignified an exit as beheading might permit. Accompanied by two ladies in waiting, she walked out in the bright May sunshine to a scaffold that had been erected on the north side of the White Tower. Strictly speaking, the sentence for a woman found guilty as she had been was to be burned alive, but Henry had enough mercy to commute this to decapitation. And instead of the usual blunt axe, she would be dispatched by a sharp blade, wielded by the expert French swordsman Jean Rombaud.

Anne was wearing a red petticoat, and a dark grey damask robe, trimmed with ermine. She gave a pious and judicious speech of farewell, in which she made no admission of guilt but affirmed her loyalty to Henry. It is said that Rombaud was so moved by her dignity that he played a merciful trick, asking, "Where is my sword?" to distract her before instantly taking her head off with one clean blow. Among those who saw her death was her old suitor, Thomas Wyatt, who gazed in horror through the small window of his prison cell in the White Tower. He later wrote a mournful poem about the execution, which ends with the words *circa Regna tonat*: About the throne, the thunder roars.

MARY, THE OTHER BOLEYN SISTER

Before King Henry VIII relentlessly pursued Anne Boleyn, it was her sister, Mary, that sparked his interest. Following affairs in France–King Francois I referred to her as his "English mare"–Mary returned to England and joined the court as a maid of honor to Queen Catherine of Aragon.

Her romance with the King lasted between two and five years, but Mary enjoyed none of the wealth, fame or power that other mistresses were used to. Two years after the affair began, she married William Carey and gave birth to two children, one of which, a boy, supposedly bore a striking resemblance to the King. Following Carey's death, Mary married William Stafford without the King's permission and was ousted from the court. She lived the rest of her life estranged from her family.

Anne witnessed how little Mary gained from the affair, so when Henry came courting, she refused him. She held out for nearly six years, until the King's marriage to Catherine was annulled and she could rightfully marry him and take the throne.

CHAPTER 10

BLOODY MARY AND THE FIRST OF THE SMITHFIELD BURNINGS

1555

Newgate Prison, early morning. The guards came and kicked awake John Rogers, who was always a heavy sleeper. He had been held prisoner here since January 1554, when the new Catholic Bishop of London, Edmund Bonner, condemned this gentle middle-aged scholar to languish in the darkness and filth with thieves and murderers. The guards jeered at Rogers, and told him that he was about to be burned to death. "If it be so," he said, "I need not tie my points." (That is, lace up his shirt.) Rogers asked for a final talk with his beloved wife Adriana; the request was refused. But as he was led through the streets from Newgate to Smithfield, he caught sight of Adriana among the crowds, surrounded by their ten older children and holding their eleventh to her breast.

In Smithfield, Rogers was tied to the stake and was given a final chance to repent by a local sheriff. His crime was to have renounced Catholicism and embraced the Church of England. More offensive still to the Catholic regime that now ruled the country, he had collaborated on a new translation of the Bible into English—the first, it was often said, to be directly translated from Hebrew and Greek. Under the brief reign of Edward VI—an invalid child-king, who held the throne as a puppet of Edward Seymour, Duke

⟨ *The Death of Archbishop Thomas Cranmer*, by Kronheim, from
Foxe's Book of Martyrs, 1887

Depiction of the execution of John Rogers at Smithfield, London, 1555

of Somerset, and others from his tenth to his sixteenth years—Rogers's Anglicanism had been neither a crime nor a career disadvantage.

Indeed, during those six years England had become an unequivocally Protestant nation. Thomas Cranmer, Archbishop of Canterbury, published his *Book of Common Prayer* in 1549, laying out the format for the Protestant mass. Waves of angry iconoclasm left many churches stripped of their remaining popish statues and stained glass windows; throughout England, elaborate stone altars were replaced with austere wooden tables. That same year, the first Act of Uniformity was passed, establishing the practices outlined in the *Book of Common Prayer* as the only legal form of worship in England and levying a fine against those who did not attend mass at least once a week.

The status of the Church of England was cemented. It was all good news for Rogers, who returned from a long stay on the Continent, and, in 1550, was awarded the livings of two London churches, St. Margaret Moses and

St. Sepulchre. In 1551 he had been given a senior post at St. Paul's, and was soon appointed a lecturer in Divinity there.

Then, in April 1553, the boy king Edward died of consumption and—to the dread of most Protestants—his Catholic half-sister Mary came to the throne. The daughter of Henry VIII, she was the first woman to claim rule of England successfully. It was not merely a return to Catholic forms of worship that the English Protestants feared; they were well aware that Mary had deep bonds with Spain and also wanted to put the country under the governance of Pope Julius III in Rome.

Displaying greater courage than tact, Rogers made his first sermon of her reign a passionate condemnation of the Church of Rome. On August 16, 1553, he was arrested. Towards the end of January, he faced a commission appointed by Mary's religious advisor and leading minister Cardinal Reginald Pole. Rogers steadfastly denied the Christian character of the Roman Church. He was sentenced to public execution by fire.

"Thou art an heretic," the sheriff said, as he prepared to set off the blaze. "That shall be known at the Day of Judgment," Rogers replied. "Well, I will never pray for thee," the sheriff shot back. Rogers remained calm and forgiving: "But I will pray for thee."

And so the fires started. Londoners were usually all too keen to cheer at executions and mock the condemned, but on this day the crowd was respectfully quiet, almost silent save for discreet expressions of sympathy for Rogers's fate and admiration of the uncomplaining courage with which he was meeting death. One eyewitness remarked that he appeared to be "washing his hands in the flame as he was burning."

Within the next few weeks, another six Protestants were burned at the stake, including the Oxford Martyrs: leading churchmen Nicholas Ridley, Hugh Latimer and the Archbishop of Canterbury, Thomas Cranmer. Latimer's brave speech to his friend as they awaited the flames has become immortal: "Be of good comfort, Master Ridley, and play the man. We shall this day light such a candle by God's grace in England as I trust shall never be put out."

Left: *Mary I, Queen of England, second wife of Felipe II*, by Anthonis Mor, 1554
Right: *Portrait of Philip II*, by Titian, 1551, sent to Mary during marriage negotiations.

By the time of Queen Mary's death three years later, more than 280 Protestants had been executed—at least 220 men, 60 women. Some estimates place the number of Marian Martyrs as high as 300. No wonder that the whole of England rejoiced sincerely at having a new and Protestant queen, Mary's half-sister, Elizabeth.

"Bloody Mary" has gone down in popular memory as a vindictive, paranoid tyrant, so it is hardly surprising that in more recent times novelists, playwrights and historians have tried to find excuses for her incendiary ways. It is undeniably true that her life was wretched. The daughter of Henry VIII and his first wife, Catherine of Aragon, she was a half-Spanish child who, after long years of personal tuition by the eminent Spanish philosopher Juan Luis Vives, stubbornly denied her father's right to be head of the Church, until it was pointed out to her forcefully how dangerous this might be. As a young woman, she seems to have craved for true romantic love rather than her series of short-lived political betrothals to assorted foreign princes. At the age of twenty-eight she had resigned herself to being a spinster: "While my father lives I shall be only the Lady Mary, the most unhappy lady in Christendom."

Mary did eventually marry, to Philip II of Spain, in July 1554. The marriage was Mary's attempt to quickly produce an heir and secure that her Protestant half-sister, Elizabeth, would not succeed her. (Furthur fearing rebellion from her sister's Protestant supporters, Mary locked Elizabeth the Tower.) Only a year earlier, Mary's own ascension had been the matter of intense debate. Her younger half-brother, King Edward VI, had disinherited both of his sisters before his death, passing the Crown to a cousin, Lady Jane Grey. It took an act of Parliament for Mary to assume her place on the throne.

For Philip, marriage into the Tudor Dynasty was a purely diplomatic arrangement, and he neglected her rudely. Mary's health was poor, and she suffered both in body and mind from a phantom pregnancy soon after her marriage. Matters came to a head for her when Parliament refused to have Philip crowned King of England. Soon, she took it into her troubled head that the failure of her marriage was due to Divine anger at the fact that the English were still playing the part of heretics. And so the burnings began.

If the Almighty was appeased by the rich smoke from Smithfield, he showed little sign. In January 1558, England suffered the humiliating loss of Calais to France, a prized possession left over from the Hundred Years' War. England's prestige, which had been steadily mounting, took a precipitate dive, and the English people held Mary responsible. Increasingly ill and dejected, she reconciled with Elizabeth, now out of the Tower. When Mary died of influenza, on November 17, 1558, her heart and bowels were cut out and buried in the Chapel Royal in St. James's Palace, while the rest of her body was interred at Westminster Abbey. Some said it was a suitable fate for a woman who had always been fatally divided between England and Spain.

CHAPTER 11

ELIZABETH I KNIGHTS FRANCIS DRAKE

4 APRIL 1581

The scene took place upon a ship moored on the Thames at Deptford, and it has been pictured in countless history books for children. The dashing Francis Drake, about forty years old but still youthful-looking and full of vigor, had returned to England just seven months earlier, after the epic three-year voyage that made him the first English captain to circumnavigate the globe, kneels before his Queen and is made a knight. It is an emblem of the flowering of the nation's new-found wealth, power and brilliance under the last of the Tudor monarchs; the emblematic beginning of a Golden Age, launched on a ship called the *Golden Hind*. A seductive picture, and, like many such pictures, not altogether accurate.

We need to make at least one small correction to the scene: Drake was not knighted by the Queen—it was the Victorians who invented that detail—but by a visiting French diplomat, Côme Clausse, Lord Marchaumont. Queen Elizabeth wanted the implicit approval of France for this act of ennoblement, which was largely a reward for Drake's ferocious and vastly profitable plundering of Spanish ports and ships. The Queen's half-share of Drake's recent looting was the equivalent of all her other incomes for the year.

‹ *Queen Elizabeth Knighting Sir Francis Drake on board the Golden Hind at Deptford, April 4, 1581.* Engraving by F. Fraenkel after drawing by J. Gilbert.

Sir Francis Drake Wearing the Drake Jewel or Drake Pendant at his Waist, by Marcus Gheeraerts the Younger, 1591

To the hostile eyes of Spain, who knew Drake as "the Master Thief of the unknown world," or more simply as "El Draque" (The Dragon), Elizabeth was in effect lending her seal of approval to the most dangerous pirate of the age. Philip II had put a price on Drake's head of what would today be more than six million dollars. Outright war with Spain was still seven years in the future, but this gesture would anger Philip, and Elizabeth knew it. But she had a sense of gratitude to Drake which made her gild the prize of a knighthood with a far more personal favor. Elizabeth gave him a specially commissioned piece of two-faced jewelry. On the one side was an engraving of two busts—a regal lady (presumably meant to be Elizabeth herself) and an African man (presumably a slave). On the other was a portrait of Elizabeth by the finest artist of the age, Nicholas Hilliard. Drake treasured this gift above all his other possessions, and when he later had his own portrait painted, he made sure that it was prominently displayed. Today, the Drake Jewel can be seen in the National Maritime Museum.

Drake's reputation as a national hero and the most important English naval warrior (an honorific without challenge before Admiral Horatio Nelson), was sealed by two key accomplishments: the great circumnavigation of 1577 to 1580, and his part in defeating the Spanish Armada during its attempted invasion of England in 1588. There can be no doubt of Drake's courage, resourcefulness and brilliance, above all as a navigator; some have called him the greatest navigator since Magellan. But hand in glove with those virtues were qualities that are much less attractive from a modern point of view. If the Spanish despised Drake as a pirate, we are more repelled by the earliest years of his seafaring career, when he took part in one of the English slaving voyages to West Africa, led by his second cousin John Hawkins.

Drake's landing in California in 1579

Drake's origins are not well known, as he was not part of a great family; his humble birth in a devoutly Protestant Devon farming family was often remarked on by higher-born rivals, who thought that he had risen too far, too fast. Most sources state that he was born in 1540, though the date is conjectural. He served a mercantile apprenticeship to a childless man, who left Drake a small ship upon his death, but Drake's career did not really gather momentum until 1567, when he joined Hawkins on that slaving trip. Spanish forces attacked, and Drake's company lost all but two ships. His lifelong hatred for Spain was born.

In 1570 and 1571, Drake made two profitable voyages to the West Indies and compounded these successes with a series of raids against Spanish ports in the Caribbean; one of his victories was the conquest of the port of Nombre de Dios on the Isthmus of Panama. He returned to England laden with treasure.

Noting Drake's exceptional prowess, Elizabeth sent him on a secret mission against Spanish colonies in South America in 1577. Spain was harvesting the astonishing wealth of its possessions in the New World; Drake's business was to harvest the harvesters. Though he did not know it at the outset, this would be the start of his three-year trip around the world. He set sail with five ships, but weather during the Atlantic crossing proved lethal, and he had soon lost all but one of them, the *Pelican*. Renamed the *Golden Hind*—after the female deer on the crest of the ship's patron—it reached the Pacific in

English ships and the Spanish Armada, August 1588, by an unknown artist

October 1578; Drake had become the first Englishman to navigate the Straits of Magellan and reach the unknown ocean. He sailed north, in search of a passage back to the Atlantic, and eventually reached the land that is now California and claimed it for Elizabeth under the name of Nova Albion. Then he set off across the Pacific, to the Moluccas, Java and ultimately past the Cape of Good Hope. The *Golden Hind* reached England in September 1580, stuffed with spices and precious metals.

In 1585 Drake undertook another profitable series of raids against Spanish cities in the West Indies and on the coast of Florida. But the next phase of his career was more directly patriotic. Full-scale war with Spain was now imminent, so, in 1587, Drake struck a massive preemptive blow by sailing into the harbor at Cádiz and destroying at least thirty Spanish galleons. The British historian Simon Schama has provocatively described this raid as "a sixteenth-century Pearl Harbor." A year later, when the Armada of some 130 galleons sailed against England, Drake was vice-Admiral of the triumphant English fleet. The much-repeated story about Drake's impeccably cool blood at the time—he is said to have insisted on finishing a game of bowls at Plymouth before setting sail—is a myth. But he had reason to be confident of victory. English ships were faster, easier to maneuver, and had far more advanced weapons—they could fire a complete fusillade once an hour, where Spain's ships could only discharge once a day.

The Armada was duly defeated, with the accidental help of high winds that made it impossible for the Spanish either to advance or to land soldiers on English soil. Good Protestant Englishmen saw the hand of God in this triumph over a Catholic enemy. "He blew with His winds, and they were scattered," went the popular saying about the fortuitous "Protestant Wind." It was a decisive moment in the balance of European forces, and some historians have seen it as the point at which Britain began its growth into what was, by the nineteenth century, the world's greatest naval power. (The term "British Empire" was first used in Elizabeth's reign by her court astrologer, Dr. John Dee.)

Drake might easily have rested on his laurels. But the man's overreaching ambition would not let him pause, and he set off on what was to be his final expedition to the West Indies. This proved disastrous. He caught "the bloody flux," dysentery, and died on January 28, 1596. The famed sailor was buried at sea. Already a mythic figure in his own lifetime, Drake began to generate myths for many years after his demise. The most romantic of them is the story of Drake's Drum, held in Buckland Abbey, his final English home. When the nation is once again in danger of invasion, the story goes, Drake's drum will sound again.

CHAPTER 12.

THE COURTSHIP OF ELIZABETH AND ESSEX
MAY 1587

Robert Devereux, Earl of Essex, was a strikingly handsome youth of not quite twenty. He was tall, auburn-haired, open in manner, boyish in spirits and charming to both men and women. In spite of his youth, he had already proved his courage in battle during the war with the Netherlands, where he had been knighted for gallantry by his stepfather, Robert Dudley, Earl of Leicester, a longtime favorite of the Queen. Apart from the occasional bout of melancholy, which would send him off to bed for days at a time, his only apparent flaw was his want of money—he was the poorest Earl in the nation. On his return to England from the war, Robert presented himself at court. Elizabeth was smitten. Gossips whispered that it was love at first sight.

Throughout the month of May, 1587, the two of them were hardly to be found apart. By day they talked and flirted or rode through the parks of London. He was universally recognized as her new favorite. At night they dined and laughed at Whitehall, and heard music until all their company had retired. Then, alone, they stayed up through the night, playing cards and other games. "My Lord cometh not to his own lodging till birds sing in the morning," wrote an observer in the court. It was an idyll, probably the happiest time in her life. There was just one discordant note in this giddy

Robert Devereux, 2nd Earl of Essex, Nicholas Hilliard, 1587

courtship. Elizabeth was fifty-three — by the standards of her time, an old woman.

To most observers, this unbalanced affair would have seemed merely calculating on the part of Essex, and self-deluded folly on the part of Elizabeth. The fine young man declared his "worship — his adoration — his love," both in person and in a series of eloquent letters that she read and reread with unflagging pleasure. She rewarded him in numerous ways, most profitably by giving him the right to take a share of the taxes levied on the import of sweet wines. He was rich overnight.

Yet it would be rash to conclude that Essex was simply playing the part of courtly lover in a cynical way. In her earlier years, Elizabeth had been beautiful and intensely charismatic; some of the most powerful men in Europe had been fascinated by her, and she used her attractiveness shrewdly for personal gain. In old age she would become grotesque: painting her face thick with cosmetics, hiding her grey hair under one of thirty wigs, shunning mirrors and demanding daily affirmations of her beauty from servants and nobles alike. But at fifty-three, she still retained just enough of her former romantic allure to make Essex partly believe his own amorous words.

Their courtship took place just months before the most significant military event of her reign: the defeat of the Spanish Armada in 1588. It is often said that Elizabeth's forty-four year reign falls into two parts: the three decades that preceded the Armada and the fifteen years that followed it. Thirty years, that is, of the intensely hard work needed to bring a remarkable degree of unity, peace and (relatively speaking) freedom to what had been a wretchedly divided nation; and then the massive explosion of energies in almost every field of endeavor that made the last decade and a half seem like England's Golden Age.

Above all, it was a time of sudden flowering of the greatest writers England had known since the death of Chaucer. In addition to the playwrights whose

Procession portrait of Elizabeth I of England, to Robert Peake the Elder, c. 1600

works are still performed in the twenty-first century—Christopher Marlowe, Ben Jonson and William Shakespeare—there were regiments of poets, translators, writers of prose epics and early novelists: Sir Philip Sidney, Edmund Spenser, John Donne, Thomas Nashe, Thomas Chapman. Music flourished, and at least four of England's greatest composers—Orlando Gibbons, William Byrd, John Dowland and Thomas Campion—worked under Elizabeth's reign, often with her patronage. And though many of the day's leading artists were guests from other nations, Elizabethan England did produce one native talent of the first order: the portrait-painter Nicholas Hilliard. England had never quite known such a constellation of genius.

For Elizabeth herself, those national glories were overshadowed by her bitter awareness of old age and by the heartbreak of her affair with Essex. Their relationship has been called a tragedy, and not without reason. It reached a head in 1599. Essex had been dispatched to Ireland to put down yet another rebellion, and had set off with a large army and the noisy acclaim of London's citizens—he was always popular with the London crowd. But he bungled the job, through a combination of poor strategy, hesitation and bad luck. Though he had vowed, in a flowery private letter to Elizabeth, that he would defeat the rebel leader, Tyrone, or die in the attempt, he was eventually forced to make an anti-climactic treaty with the Irish. Then, contrary to orders, he came back to England, made his way to the Queen's

residence at Nonsuch Palace and stormed into her bedroom. There he found Elizabeth, unpainted, without gown or wig, with her gray hair dropping over her astonished face.

He was arrested and imprisoned for almost a year. Eventually he was tried and found guilty of incompetence, but after entering an impassioned bid for mercy he was allowed to return to his house and await her Majesty's pleasure. Shortly afterwards, he heard that she had decided to take away his right to farm wine taxes, so sending him back into poverty. He exploded with rage, and, when someone referred to "her Majesty's conditions," he shouted the fatal words: "Her conditions are as crooked as her carcass!" In his rage, he grew desperate, and he gathered several hundred followers to rebel, assuming that his popularity among Londoners was so great that thousands would rally. He miscalculated. Almost no one joined his throng, and by the afternoon most of his followers slipped away. He surrendered to the Queen's troops, and was sent to the Tower.

Queen Elizabeth I presiding over Parliament, engraving, 1608

Once again he was put to trial, this time for his life, on February 19, 1601. Thanks in part to a brilliant speech for the prosecution by Francis Bacon, Essex was found guilty of treason and condemned to death. Even at this point, Elizabeth had it within her power to issue a pardon and—after a tactful interval—to bring Essex back into her circle. But her heart was hardened, and one of the qualities that had hardened it was her vanity.

She was notorious for her hesitations before any great decision; this time she barely hesitated at all. On February 23rd, she sent a message that the execution should be postponed. On the 24th she changed her mind and told the executioners to proceed. The axe fell on Essex's head on the morning of February 25th. It took three strokes before the head, which had once so charmed the Queen, was severed from the body.

1. *A Little Prince Likely in Time to Bless a Royal Throne*, by E. Blair Leighton, 1904 **2.** *David Garrick as Richard III*, by William Hogarth, 1745, Walker Art Gallery, Liverpool **3.** *The Courtship of Anne Boleyn*, by Emanuel Gottlieb Leutze, 1846, Smithsonian American Art Museum **4.** *Execution of Lady Jane Grey*, by Paul Delaroche, 1833, National Gallery, London **5.** *Execution of Mary, Queen of Scots*, by Abel de Pujol, 1800s, Musée des Beaux-Arts Valenciennes; **6.** *The Death of Queen Elizabeth I*, by Paul Delaroche, 1828, Louvre Museum

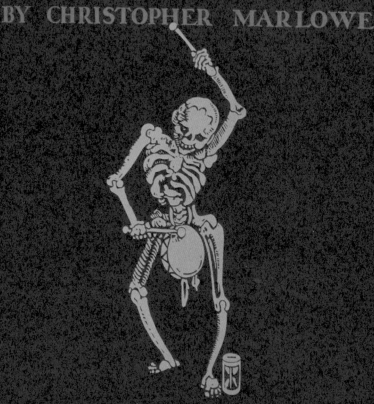

W.P.A. FEDERAL THEATRE PRESENTS

FAUSTUS

BY CHRISTOPHER MARLOWE

MAXINE ELLIOTT'S THEATRE

CHAPTER 13.

THE KILLING OF CHRISTOPHER MARLOWE IN DEPTFORD

30 MAY 1593

It was, so they said, an instant death. The dagger went in straight above the poet's right eye, and Christopher Marlowe's lifeless body fell to the tavern floor. Marlowe was only 29 years old, and at the height of his powers. In the space of about six years, he had become the most successful playwright of his age — although another young writer, William Shakespeare, was beginning to look like a serious rival.

For some of his contemporaries, however, this was a death richly deserved. Dark rumours circulated about Marlowe. Just ten days earlier, on May 20, 1593, he had been ordered to appear before the Privy Council to answer charges of heresy. Many suspected — and they were almost certainly right — that he had been deeply involved in spying and had been a key agent of Sir Thomas Walsingham, Queen Elizabeth's spy-master. He had been accused of counterfeiting coins in the Netherlands, and it was said by his enemies that he had bragged "all those that love not Tobacco or Boys are fool." Thanks to his play about Doctor Faustus, the man who sells his soul to the devil, Marlowe had even been suspected of witchcraft. So generation after generation has wondered: Was Marlowe simply the accidental victim of a drunken brawl or had he been murdered?

‹ Poster for a production of the play *Faustus* by Christopher Marlowe

Portrait of a 21-year-old man, thought to be Christopher Marlowe, 1585

The record is tantalizingly patchy, though a full coroner's report of the fatal day was found in the early twentieth century. The inquest found Marlowe's killer, Ingram Frizer, not guilty of premeditated murder, and accepted that he acted in self-defense after Marlowe drew his dagger during a bitter argument about the bill for that day's drunken carousing at a Deptford inn. But Frizer was a known member of Walsingham's secret service, as were his two companions in the company that day, Nicholas Skeres and Robert Poley. There were other strange circumstances. Was the not guilty verdict a cover-up? Had Marlowe in fact been assassinated by his fellow spies?

A violent death made an apt ending for a man whose dramatic career had thrived on savage, bloody and unnatural acts. Besides some poems and translations, Marlowe's career rests on the half-dozen full-length stage plays he managed to complete: *Dido, Queen of Carthage*, based on Virgil's epic poem the *Aeneid*; the two parts of *Tamburlaine the Great*, probably staged around 1587, and now considered one of the earliest flowerings of the mature Elizabethan stage; *The Jew of Malta*, with its deliciously evil villain Barabbas; *Edward the Second*, a brutal play about English history; and *The Massacre at Paris*, a comparably brutal work about the Saint Bartholemew's Day Massacre of 1572. Finally, and most famously, there was his masterpiece *The Tragicall Historie of the Life and Death of Doctor Faustus*, based on German narratives about the learned man who sold his soul to the Devil in return for occult knowledge and worldly power.

The groundlings, the poorest of theatergoers, loved these flashy, action-packed plays, which made a star of the actor Edward Alleyn, a powerful man who appears to have played the leading roles of Tamburlaine, Barabbas and Faustus. Yet it seems possible that the profession of dramatist was no more than a part-time one for Marlowe; that his true career was covert.

84

Christopher Marlow was baptised in Canterbury on February 26, 1564, which makes him just a couple of months older than Shakespeare. Marlowe's father was a shoemaker, Shakespeare's a glove-maker. The young Marlowe was sent to the King's School, Canterbury and then to Corpus Christi, Cambridge; unlike Shakespeare, Marlowe was one of the so-called University Wits. He earned his B.A. in 1584, but when it came time for his Master's in 1587, there was some objection from the university, until the Privy Council stepped in, cited his "good service" to the Queen and made the degree award go ahead. It is still not certain what this "good service" might have been, but modern historian Charles Nicholl has discovered documents which prove that Marlowe began to receive very substantial payments while still an undergraduate, likely from Sir Francis Walsingham. In short, Marlowe was probably a spy for his entire adult life.

At the time of his death, Marlowe was awaiting trial for a charge of "heresy." Earlier in the month, the authorities had raided the lodgings of Marlowe's fellow playwright Thomas Kyd, where they had found a document expressing terrible heresies: probably arguments for atheism. Under examination, which may have included torture, Kyd had told his captors that the document belonged to Marlowe. This was damning, as was the rumour that Marlowe had been a member of the "School of Night," a circle of poets, thinkers and (so the story went) occultists who gathered around Henry Percy, the "Wizard Earl" of Northumberland. Modern scholars mostly agree that the School of Night did not really exist.

Marlowe's death shocked the small world of London's theater. Shakespeare paid tributes to his rival in *As You Like It*: The couplet "Dead Shepherd, now I find thy saw of might/'Whoever loved that loved not at first sight?'" tips the hat to a line from Marlowe's long poem "Hero and Leander."

There have been endless speculations about how Marlowe might have developed had he lived into his thirties and forties. Might he have been as great as Shakespeare? Greater? One conspiracy theory holds that Marlowe actually *was* the author of the later plays attributed to the man from Stratford-upon-Avon—that Marlowe was not killed at all, but spirited away to the Continent, where he wrote his works in secrecy, using his old pal Shakespeare as a front. As Marlowe might have put it: Those who believe such toys are fools.

CHAPTER 14

SHAKESPEARE AND THE OPENING OF THE GLOBE THEATRE

JULY 1599

The winter of 1598–9 had been bitterly cold; so cold that the Thames froze and the job of building a new theater for the acting company the Lord Chamberlain's Men had been delayed by months. It was hard for the workmen to dig deep enough through the iron-hard earth for proper foundations. But the company had no choice but to go ahead, because a 21-year lease on their old theater—known, prosaically, as "The Theatre," in Shoreditch, north of the Thames—had expired at the end of the previous year, and their landlord, Giles Allen, had gone back on his agreement to let the company stay there. So just after Christmas, while the owner was away, the Chamberlain's men armed themselves with clubs and knives, marched through the streets of Shoreditch, and rapidly tore down The Theatre.

By nightfall on December 28, the old frame of The Theatre was reduced to timbers, which were loaded on to carts and dragged away by horse-drawn carts to a waterfront warehouse on Peter Street, near Bridewall Stairs. When the ice finally thawed in the late spring of 1599, these timbers were shipped across the river to Southwark and used to build the grandest theater London had ever seen: The Globe.

< *The Last Kiss of Romeo and Juliet*, by Francesco Hayez, 1823

The Globe Theatre

The first London theater built by actors for actors, the Globe was a fitting home for the Lord Chamberlain's Men, who were widely agreed to have the finest actors of the day, above all the charismatic Richard Burbage, an Elizabethan superstar. Partly open to the sky, it was a large amphitheater-like structure, about 100 feet in diameter and 30 feet high; it could hold up to 3,000 spectators, either seated in its three stories or standing in the arena. A large apron-style stage thrust out into the standing crowd, bringing them extremely close to the action. Along with their new theater and impressive company, the Chamberlain's Men also had a popular, and already wealthy resident playwright: William Shakespeare.

In the summer of 1599, Shakespeare was thirty-five: an advanced age for the Elizabethans, who tended to die young even if they escaped plague (at the height of the plague of 1593, 1,000 Londoners died every week) or violence (in 1595, the city was in such a state of riot and anarchy that martial law was imposed). To the theater-going masses, he was less familiar as a playwright than as an actor, now specializing in older characters—soon, he would be playing the ghost of Hamlet's father. To the elite, he was highly regarded as a poet; his narrative poem *Venus and Adonis*, published in 1593, was greeted with rapture, while another poem, *The Passionate Pilgrim*, was one of the best-selling books of 1599. Inside his company, Shakespeare was regarded as a man with an enviable flair for pleasing the grubby, stinking groundlings, who could only afford to sit on the theater's floor.

Richard Burbage

His breakthrough had come seven years earlier, when *Harry the Sixth*, as it was then known, was the hit of the 1592 season, seen by more than 10,000 people. A string of other successes—such as the horrific *Titus Andronicus*—had brought him enough money that he had been able to buy a ten percent share in the Globe. In all, he had either written or collaborated on about eighteen plays and was the most experienced playwright in the land.

Over the last 250 years, Shakespeare's reputation has grown to such cosmic dimensions that it is often hard to realize that his contemporaries saw him very differently. There was plenty of money to be made in the theater, true, but it was a disreputable trade, seen by Puritans as being roughly on a par with brothel-keeping or bear-baiting—and the area around the Globe was rich in such rival entertainments. The theaters were frequently closed down, and a company could only thrive if it managed to find a powerful patron, like the rival Lord Admiral's Men, who were based a stone's throw away from the site of the Globe, in the Rose Theatre. Shakespeare himself had begun his theatrical career acting with the Lord Strange's Men, sometime between 1587 and 1592. He published his earliest plays in 1594, less in the hope of royalties than to protect his copyright, since this was a notorious age of literary piracy. By 1598 his name was enough of a draw to be put on the title pages. He was beginning to be a local celebrity.

Offstage, "Sweet Master Shakespeare," as he was called, was exceptionally gentle in his ways. England's most famous playwright did not greatly enjoy drinking and making merry with his colleagues, but that may have been because his only opportunity to read and write would have been in the evenings, as plays were staged in the afternoons. Both the elite and the mob enjoyed his tales of love, and he was known as the "English Ovid," after the Roman poet who wrote the *Amores*. Yet little is known of his love life in

Mr. WILLIAM
SHAKESPEARES
COMEDIES,
HISTORIES, &
TRAGEDIES.

Published according to the True Originall Copies.

LONDON
Printed by Isaac Iaggard, and Ed. Blount. 1623

Title page of the first folio of
William Shakespeare's Complete
Works, 1623

these years, when he was living in effect as a bachelor, with his wife and children in Stratford-upon-Avon, save for a mildly risqué story. Richard Burbage, it goes, arranged a romantic rendezvous while playing the part of Richard II. Wily Shakespeare took Burbage's place while he was busy on stage, and left a message for the actor that "William the Conqueror came before Richard II."

Had Shakespeare died on the day the Globe opened—probably with a production of his *Henry V*, which includes a reference to the "Wooden O" of the new theater—how would he be thought of today? Certainly not as the demigod into which the Romantics turned him near the start of the nineteenth century. Besides his poems, he was thus far the author of the three action-packed, crowd-pleasing history plays about Henry VI, the horror show of *Titus*, a rather academic squib entitled *Love's Labour's Lost*, as well as a few better, stranger comedies like *The Merchant of Venice*, the beautiful fantasy of *A Midsummer Night's Dream*, and the flop *Two Gentlemen of Verona*. Hints of the mature Shakespeare had begun to emerge in other plays: *Romeo and Juliet*, *Richard II*, *Richard III*, all highly innovative. It is an impressive achievement, but not nearly enough to establish the glover's son from Warwickshire as the greatest Western writer since Homer.

That astonishing transformation from the talented to the titanic began with the opening of the Globe. The new theater became Shakespeare's personal musical instrument. Here, he achieved something that none of his contemporaries had so far managed—plays that delighted both the mob and the elite. Another boon came from the rise of a generation of talented boy players who could take the parts of women (it was considered improper and immodest for Elizabethan women to work in the bawdy world of the theater). Now, Shakespeare could create female roles of unprecedented complexity and realism. His first plays for the Globe were probably *Henry V*, *Julius Caesar* and *As You Like It*, a play which contains the line "All the world's a stage," a free translation of the Latin motto hung over the Globe's entrance, *Totus mundum agit histrionem*. Then the master works—comedies, tragedies and plays that cannot be classified—sprang from his pen: *Twelfth Night, Hamlet, Othello, Macbeth, King Lear*. English drama had never been so psychologically exact, so compelling, so rich in verbal music, so all-embracing.

The first Globe burned down on June 29, 1613, when a special effect of a cannon firing went badly wrong during a performance of one of Shakespeare's last plays, a collaboration with playwright John Fletcher, called *Henry VIII*. Shakespeare lived long enough to see it rebuilt in 1614, but died just two years later, an old man of 52. Like all the other theaters in London, the second Globe was closed down in 1642, when the Puritans began their ascendancy at the start of the Civil Wars. That appeared to be the end of the story, until 1997, when a replica of Shakespeare's theater opened to the public, about 750 feet from the original site. This development was the brainchild of the American director and actor Sam Wanamaker, and has proved a great success. In the summer months, plays by Shakespeare and others are performed in much the way they would have been performed to Elizabethans, though audiences today are cleaner and much more polite. Simply gazing at the building is enough to make one marvel how the greatest dramatic poetry of all time rose from a district notorious for violence, cruelty and profound squalor. It is a wonder.

CHAPTER 15.

GUY FAWKES AND THE GUNPOWDER PLOT
5 NOVEMBER 1605

The first torture was simply to be put in manacles and hanged up on the cell wall, deep inside the Tower of London. It caused the prisoner dreadful pain, but it was not enough to wring a full confession from him. So they moved him to the rack—a rectangular wooden frame, slightly tilted at one end and equipped with wheels and ratchets. The prisoner's arms were fastened above his head, and his feet fastened to the base. Then the torturer began to turn his wheel, notch by notch. Even this big, tough man now began to scream with the pain, though the screams were not loud enough to cover the sharp popping noises that came as, one by one, his joints cracked apart. To be broken on the rack is one of the greatest agonies a prisoner can suffer. Yet worse was to come. The punishers put torches to the howling man's legs and stomach and chest, raising angry welts of burned skin. Using specially designed pincers, they tore out the nails on his fingers and toes. It is a wonder he managed to resist even for as long as a few minutes. Astonishingly, it took almost two full days for Guy Fawkes to crack and name his fellow conspirators in the Gunpowder Plot.

Strictly speaking, torture was not permitted under English law. But there was a legal loophole: the King could invoke Royal Prerogative, and James I did

Eight of the Thirteen Conspirators, by Crispijn van de Passe. Fawkes is third from the right.

not scruple to call on his right when it came to the men who had come very close to murdering him a few hours earlier. His orders on the morning of November 6, 1605 were clear: "The gentler tortours are to be first used unto him, *et sic per gradus ad ima tenditur* (and so by stages increased to the harshest), and so God speed your good work." So, under the direction of Sir William Waad, Lieutenant of the Tower, Fawkes suffered the torments of the damned. When it was all over, and he was given a pen with which to sign his confession, he could hardly hold it. The signature is so jagged and ill-formed as to be almost illegible.

It was his loyalty to the Catholic faith that had led Guy Fawkes to the Tower. He was born in Yorkshire in 1570, and though his father—a successful Proctor, or lawyer—belonged to the Church of England, his mother and her family members were all pious Catholic recusants. Guy was eight when his father died; his mother soon took a new husband, who was also Catholic. Once he reached adulthood, Fawkes went to Europe, where he fought for the Catholic Spanish (who called him "Guido") against the Protestant Dutch as part of the Eighty Years' War. In 1603, he petitioned the King of Spain to launch another Armada against England, dethrone James and establish a Catholic monarchy. Fawkes described James as a "heretic" who wanted "to have all of the Papist sect driven out of England." He was received politely, but Spain was in no mood to wage another war.

When Fawkes returned to England, Catholic friends introduced him to Robert Catesby, who was putting together a conspiracy to assassinate James and replace him with the Catholic Princess Elizabeth, third in the line to the throne—and just nine years old. There were thirteen conspirators in all; five of them convened at a fatal meeting on May 20, 1604, at the Duck and Drake pub on the Strand. It was agreed that Fawkes would adopt the pseudonym "John Johnson," and pass himself off

King James I of England and VI of Scotland, by Daniel Mytens, 1621

as the servant of another plotter, Thomas Wintour, who had access to the home of the Keeper of the King's Wardrobe.

It was a simple plan: When the King and his ministers assembled for the annual state opening of Parliament, they would be blown up. After reconnaissance, the plotters took out a lease on a storage room—an undercroft—immediately underneath the great hall in the House of Lords where Parliament met. Here, they stockpiled gunpowder and firewood. The attack was originally planned for the first session of Parliament in late July, but a plague scare meant that the opening was postponed until November 5th.

But there were leaks. An anonymous person, friendly to William Parker, Lord Monteagle, warned him to stay away from Parliament as something dreadful was going to happen. The conspirators discovered this leak, but were persuaded that Monteagle and others had treated the warning as a hoax. Not so. King James took the keenest interest and ordered his man Sir Thomas Kynvet to sweep the area. Fawkes, the plotter whose job it was to light the fuse, was discovered and arrested in the early hours of November 5th. Parliament made sure that the attempted outrage was known to all citizens as soon as possible. Bonfires of celebration were lit all across London that night.

Fawkes's first interrogation was by the King's Privy Council. He gave his name as John Johnson, but otherwise admitted his guilt so fearlessly

The Execution of Guy Fawkes, by Claes Jansz Visscher, c. 1606

that even King James was impressed, and said that Fawkes had shown "a Roman resolution." But Fawkes stubbornly refused to name any of his fellow conspirators. It took the rack to tear that information from him, on November 8th.

On January 17, 1606, eight of the thirteen conspirators were taken to Westminster Hall for trial. Fawkes now pleaded "Not Guilty." (He was overheard explaining to a fellow prisoner that he had entered this plea because he had not fully understood the wording of some of the charges against him.) All were found guilty of High Treason and sentenced to public execution of the most violent kind. They were to be drawn by horses, then suspended by ropes and "put to death half way between Heaven and Earth as unworthy of both." Their genitals were to be hacked off and burned before their eyes; their bowels and other inner organs pulled out, and then they would be decapitated and their remains left on the ground as fodder for the birds. On Fawkes's day of execution, he was preceded to the scaffold by several other conspirators, all of whom suffered this atrocious end. But Fawkes himself managed to struggle free of his captors and hurl himself to the ground, breaking his neck. His corpse was sliced up, and the parts sent throughout the kingdom as a warning to other potential regicides.

CHAPTER 15 GUY FAWKES

Though Catesby was the man who had masterminded the whole plot, it was Fawkes—the man caught holding the fuse—who was immediately notorious. In the new wave of anti-Catholic sentiment that washed through England, he became first a major hate figure and then, as the years passed by, a kind of familiar bogeyman, who often seemed to belong more to folklore than to history. By the twentieth century, he was so thoroughly assimilated into popular culture that it became possible to make jokes about him. Guy Fawkes, people said, was the only man ever to enter Parliament with honest intentions.

THE LEGACY OF GUY FAWKES

Remember, remember
The Fifth of November
Gunpowder, Treason and Plot
I see no reason
Why Gunpowder Treason
Should ever be forgot....

Thus the jingle that generations of English children have learned to chant, often when they are far too young to have the slightest idea about treason or even gunpowder. It is the rhyme which accompanies the revelries of what today is usually called Bonfire Night, or Fireworks Night. America's day for pyrotechnic displays and outdoor revelry is July Fourth; Britain's is November 5. Families build fires in their gardens, cook hot snacks which steam in the cold night air, and then set off rockets and bangers and Catherine wheels. Or they go to the public bonfires and firework displays—every self-respecting town and village will fund a big outdoor party that night. And on those thousands of bonfires, people burn a straw man, a Guy. (Traditionally, children would make their own Guys in early November, take them to the street and beg passers-by for money to buy fireworks: "Penny for the Guy?") The older name for this annual revelry is Guy Fawkes's Night, and it celebrates the foiling of that terrorist action more than four centuries ago.

In the last decade or so, Fawkes has returned in a new guise. The anti-hero of Alan Moore's science-fiction comic *V for Vendetta*, set in a future Britain which has become a totalitarian state, wears a Guy Fawkes mask—and succeeds in blowing up Parliament. Thanks to this comic, and the 2006 film based on it, anti-authoritarian protestors in Britain now often wear the *V for Vendetta* Fawkes mask.

CHAPTER 16

THE TRIAL AND EXECUTION OF CHARLES I

20-30 JANUARY 1649

King Charles woke at five in the morning of Tuesday, January 30, 1649 and called his aide, Sir Thomas Herbert. "I will get up," he said, "having a great work to do today." The air was bitterly cold, so he put on two warm shirts, as he did not wish his people to see him shiver and assume that he was trembling from fear. For the same motive, he ate a modest breakfast of bread and claret, lest he should feel faint from hunger, and put an orange pierced with cloves into his pocket. At ten o'clock, an officer came for him, and told him "in trembling voice" that he was expected. In the company of his favorite Bishop, William Juxon, Charles walked out of St. James's Palace and into the park, with his spaniel, Rogue, bounding around his heels.

Just ten days earlier the King had been summoned to Westminster Hall. Charles stood trial for treason—an odd notion, and a novel one, for though earlier English monarchs had been killed or overthrown, none had ever been tried in court. But Oliver Cromwell and his followers, convinced by their overwhelming military triumphs in the Civil Wars that they had God on their side, saw no paradox in the idea of a King betraying his people. The origins of the Civil Wars are so complex that they are still the subject of fierce dispute among historians, but there are three points that are fairly clear.

‹ *The execution of King Charles I* (detail), by John Weesop, 1649

Left: *Charles I, King of England at the Hunt*, by Anthony van Dyck, 1635
Right: *Oliver Cromwell*, by Robert Walker, 1649

First, Charles—who had come to the throne in 1625—was suspected not only of being soft on Catholics, but of trying quietly to steer the Church of England back towards Catholicism: He had married a French Catholic, Henrietta Maria, and appointed an Archbishop of Canterbury who was widely believed to be a secret supporter of the Pope. Second, Charles had decided to wage a costly, unpopular war against Spain—a war which ended in defeat for the British forces. Finally, and worst of all, Charles had financed those wars by levying taxes without the permission of Parliament. Those who refused to pay up could be imprisoned. Parliament read this, not without justice, as the act of a tyrant. They rebelled and armed conflict loomed.

The first of the wars between monarchy and Parliament was waged from 1642–45, ending with Charles's defeat. (They were terribly bloody wars; almost four percent of the country's population of about five million died in battle or from wounds.) The victorious Cromwell believed that Charles might be talked into agreeing to the compromise solution of a constitutional monarchy, with the king obliged to seek Parliamentary approval of his actions. But Charles proved stubborn, escaped his captors, and raised a Scottish army to fight a second war against the Parliamentary side from

1648–49. Cromwell won again and was now determined that Charles must die.

Whatever one's view of Charles's early reign, all but his worst enemies have agreed that he conducted himself with dignity at the end of his life. Friends at the trial were shocked at how pale and gaunt he appeared, with sunken eyes, newly grey hair and drawn cheeks, all accentuated by his black velvet cloak and tall black hat. He refused to acknowledge the authority of the court Cromwell had assembled, and when charged, he would not answer. He refused on

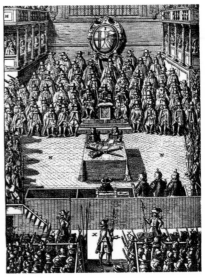

J. Nalson's Record of the Trial of Charles I, 1688

January 20th, on the 22nd, and again on the 23rd. He was warned that, by law, a prisoner who refused to plea was deemed to have pleaded guilty. But he remained eloquently defiant, for once not troubled by his chronic stammer. Finally, on January 27th, he was found guilty of being "a Tyrant, Traitor, Murderer and a Public Enemy" and condemned to death by beheading.

Charles was not ill-treated in his last three days of life, and was allowed to see his youngest children on the evening before his execution, which was to be staged outside the Banqueting House, where a black-draped scaffold was waiting. When he and his Bishop reached the House, they could see a crowd of many thousands waiting in the square. Charles could not address them directly because soldiers, armed with pikes, had been posted all around the scaffold in case of last-minute riots or rescue attempts. So Charles delivered his last formal speeches to the men gathered around the block, including two executioners dressed in naval uniform, with their faces disguised by fake beards and masks. He ended his speech by saying that he had no fear, for he was going "from a corruptible to an incorruptible crown, where no disturbance can be, no disturbance in the world."

Cromwell Lifting the Coffin-Lid and Looking at the Body of Charles I,
by Hippolyte Delaroche, 19th century

The Bishop helped him tuck his long hair up under his white satin nightcap. Charles asked his axe man if the block could be raised a little higher so that he could kneel for the fatal blow rather than lie prone, but the order had been given for him to lie so that he could be killed more easily should he struggle. "It can be no higher, Sir", the axe man said. Charles prayed for a while longer with his head tilted up to the sky, and then he lay down with his neck on the block. "Stay for the sign," he murmured. "I will, Sir, an' it please Your Majesty." A few moments later, Charles stretched out his hands as a signal that he was ready, the axe fell and the head came off with a single stroke. The executioner held it up to show the masses, but did not speak the traditional phrase, "Behold a traitor!"

One young member of the crowd recalled, "the blow I saw given, and can truly say with a sad heart, at the instant whereof, I remember well, there was such a groan by the thousands then present as I never heard before and desire

I may never hear again." There was no violent outburst from Royalists, but a number of men and women rushed around the base of the scaffold, dipping their handkerchiefs in the spilled blood, either for souvenirs or because royal blood was believed to have magical powers of healing.

Charles's body was removed, embalmed, reunited with his head by stitches, and kept in St. James's for seven days. There is a well-known tale about a strange event during that week, which only two men could have confirmed or denied. The Earl of Southampton was charged with keeping watch over the body before its burial at St. George's Chapel, Windsor Castle, on February 9th. One night, a man entered the room without noticing Southampton's presence. Southampton, it was written, recalled that the figure was "very much muffled up in his cloak and his face quite hid in it. He approached the body, considered it very attentively for some time, then shook his head and sighed out the words "Cruel Necessity!" He then departed in the same slow and concealed manner as he had come. Lord Southampton used to say that he could not distinguish anything of his face; but that by his voice and gait he took him to be Oliver Cromwell."

With Charles dead, England became a republic—known first as the Commonwealth of England, and then, with Cromwell's seizure of absolute power in 1653, the "Protectorate." It remained so until 1659—less than a year into the rule of Cromwell's successor, his son, Richard. After a year of political chaos, Charles II was restored to the throne. Under Charles II's reign, his father, Charles I, was declared a saint of the Church of England.

CHAPTER 17.

THE GREAT FIRE
2–5 SEPTEMBER, 1666

With the benefit of hindsight, it is easy to think of the Great Fire as a disaster waiting to happen. Built mostly of wood, with narrow, crammed alleys, the ancient City of London—that is to say, the area enclosed by the old Roman walls—was like a massive tinderbox, especially after a drought that had lasted since November 1665, and a freakishly hot summer that had dried the thatched roofs into so much parched kindling. In defiance of housing regulations, many of the houses were built with illegal "jetties"—new floors that thrust out from the upper levels of a building like jetties from a dock—so that each new storey stretched out further across the street, until the top levels almost touched their facing neighbors. These were the perfect conditions for spreading fires.

This was a reckless practice as well as an illegal one, but it would be wrong to think of the contemporary Londoners as entirely ignorant of risk. Small blazes were commonplace, so the City had developed a pair of emergency squads with a surprisingly good track record. A thousand so-called bellmen—members of the Watch—patrolled the streets every night, looking for sparks and flames. Meanwhile, a kind of militia known as the Trained Bands were on standby to tackle conflagrations with hoses, buckets, ladders

Great Fire of London, 1666, Victorian Engraving after Nicolaes Visscher

and "fire-hooks." Had these two teams been deployed effectively, the Great Fire might well have been prevented. If we need a villain for this story, there is one obvious candidate: Sir Thomas Bloodworth, Lord Mayor of London, who dithered while the City burned.

It began in the early hours of Sunday, September 2, at the bakery of Thomas Farriner on Pudding Lane. (Today, a plaque marks the point where the fires were started.) Farriner and his family managed to escape by climbing from the top floor of the building to the next house, but their maid, afraid of heights, was trapped and became the fire's first fatality. There was a strong east wind that night, and for the next couple of days, so the fire spread rapidly westward. Local churches began to ring their bells in warning, and the Trained Bands were soon on the scene. They wanted to contain the blaze by creating firebreaks — which called for tearing down houses — but the tenants protested bitterly. When Bloodworth arrived on the scene, he was dismissive: "Pish! A woman could piss it out!" he is remembered as saying. He refused to allow demolitions to go forward on the flimsy grounds that most of the locals were renting their rooms and the actual owners should be consulted.

It was an idiotic decision and a catastrophic one. By daybreak, the great diarist and Secretary of the Navy Samuel Pepys climbed to a high turret in

Left: *Samuel Pepys*, by J. Hayls, 1666; Right: *James II, when Duke of York*, by Peter Lely c. 1665

the Tower of London so that he could make a full survey of the fire's extent. He was shocked by what he saw. Already, some 300 houses and several churches were gone.

Pepys took a boat along the Thames to Westminster, where he reported on the disaster to Charles II. The King was appalled at Bloodworth's inaction and gave Pepys the direct order: "Spare no houses!" By the time Pepys made it back to the City, a mass evacuation had begun, and Bloodworth was a nervous wreck, "like a fainting woman." Rather than act on Charles's orders, he went home to bed. When Charles heard this, he decided to override the Mayor's traditional legal authority over the City and ordered mass demolitions. This was a wise decision and a brave one, since the City was crammed with former Republicans, including many ex-soldiers who refused to recognize his right to the Crown. Charles was risking a new rebellion, though his conduct throughout the fire was exemplary. He even joined in the actual, dangerous job of firefighting.

By Monday the work of building firebreaks had begun, but it was already too late. London Bridge, covered with houses, was already on fire, and only a gap between the buildings stopped the flames from marching straight across the Thames into Southwark. Rich merchants were scrambling to get

View of the Great Fire from the Tower Wharf area showing the Tower of London (right) and London Bridge, with St. Paul's Cathedral in the center, surrounded by flames.

their possessions out through one of the eight gates into the city; the poor simply fled. There were riots at the crammed gateways and hideous scenes of street violence due to rumors that immigrants from France and Holland had started the fires.

Somewhere among this chaos, Bloodworth simply vanished. Charles appointed his own brother, James, Duke of York, as head of the emergency efforts. James established a garrison from which teams were sent out to make firebreaks, but by now the City was a raging firestorm. Fanned by the unremitting easterly winds, flames jumped the River Fleet to the west and destroyed the luxurious shopping area of Cheapside to the north. Everyone had believed that St. Paul's would stand, but when the flames reached the old church, the vast store of papers in its crypt went up in a virtual explosion; molten lead from the roof ran through the streets. Meanwhile, to the east, the flames were coming closer to the Tower, and its stores of gunpowder. If they reached it, the explosion would have been colossal. So the guard used some of that gunpowder to make more fire-breaks outside the Tower's walls, and just about managed to contain the blaze.

It all died out on Wednesday. The east wind finally dropped, and the firebreaks near the Tower and elsewhere held. But the sorrows were not over. One hundred thousand, or roughly one sixth, of the City's inhabitants were now homeless, and there were fresh rumors of terrorism. Riots broke out among the smoking embers and when a simple-minded French watchmaker, Robert Hubert, "confessed" to having begun the fire, he was tried and hanged.

For many years it was said that the death toll of the fire was astonishingly light—perhaps only eight people. The actual figure is more likely to be in the hundreds, or thousands, since most of the dead were paupers not listed on any public records. The other legend—that the fire killed the city's rats, and so ended the plague—is equally flimsy. For one thing, the plague

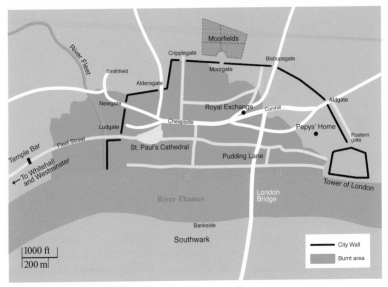

Map of damage from the Great Fire

also disappeared from other European cities at about the same time. For another, the rat-infested slums outside the walls of the City of London went unscathed by the fire.

But some good did come from the disaster: Lessons were learned — the new houses built on the sites of the old were now much more fireproof, and the City did not burn again until 1940, when the Luftwaffe's planes rained fire-bombs down on it. And one almost unknown young architect named Christopher Wren became famous and then immortal as the man who designed both the Monument to the fire and London's greatest modern building, the new St. Paul's Cathedral.

CHAPTER 18

THE FUNERAL
OF LORD NELSON

9 JANUARY 1806

When news of Horatio Nelson's death at Trafalgar finally reached England on November 6, 1805, he had been dead for 17 days. One of the first to be told was Nelson's mistress, Emma Hamilton. As she recalled it later, a man from the Admiralty named Mr. Whitby called on her. "Show him in directly," she instructed her servants. Whitby entered, pale, subdued, softly spoken. "We have gained a great Victory," he began, but she cut him off. "Never mind your Victory—my letters, give me my letters!" meaning her expected love letters from Nelson. Whitby could not bring himself to speak, but wept silently. Emma screamed and collapsed. She was incapable of speaking, crying or moving for the next ten hours.

Lady Hamilton was not alone in her suffering; the entire nation felt a sorrow almost as sharp and unappeasable as poor Emma's. "The death of Nelson was felt in England as something more than a public catastrophe: men started at the intelligence and turned pale; as if they had heard of the loss of a great friend," wrote the Poet Laureate, Robert Southey. "An object of our admiration and our affection, of our pride and our hopes, was suddenly taken from us; and it seemed as if we had never, till then, known how deeply we loved and reverenced him. What the country had lost in its great naval

---

‹ *The Death of Nelson* (detail), by Arthur Devis, 1807

Left: *Rear-Admiral Sir Horatio Nelson*, by Lemuel Francis Abbott, 1800
Right: *Lady Hamilton as a Spinster*, by George Romney, 1782-86

hero—the greatest of our own and all former times—was scarce; taken into the account of grief."

Southey did not overstate the case. Horatio Nelson was, and remains, by far the most celebrated naval hero of a nation which has traditionally taken pride in its maritime exploits. His name eclipses even those of other British mariners and admirals: Drake, Raleigh, Rodney and Howe. His greatest accomplishment was his last, a triumph over the French navy that broke Napoleonic sea-power for good. But he was already famous before he set sail on his final voyage, mainly for his bold and usually triumphant actions against France.

A native of Norfolk, Nelson had joined the Navy at the start of 1771, when he was just twelve years old. Seven years later, he had his first command. He was a superb, instinctive strategist, he won affection and respect of his men, and he was almost foolishly careless of danger and pain. His body bore witness to his courage. In 1794, he was permanently blinded in his right eye during an action in Corsica, and in 1797, he lost his right arm in the Battle of Santa Cruz de Tenerife. These wounds did not seem to diminish his attractiveness to women, and certainly not to Lady Hamilton.

The Battle of Trafalgar, by J. M. W. Turner, 1822-1824

Over the years, some voices have questioned Nelson's greatness as a man; he was known to be temperamental and insecure, with a need for recognition. Yet the intensity of the love that was felt for him, both by those who knew and served with him and by those who merely regarded him from afar as the savior of his country, is not a matter for dispute but of public record, preserved in diaries, letters and journals. By the time Nelson's body was brought back to England on December 23, everyone agreed that he should have a lavish state funeral.

Before his body was brought ashore, it was given a post-mortem examination by a Dr. William Beatty, whose forceps removed the French bullet that had fatally struck his spine. Folklore records that Nelson's remains had been preserved in a cask of brandy and raw alcohol, and for once folklore is right. (The legend that thirsty sailors took the occasional sip of his preservative fluid is probably less well founded.) Dr. Beatty's examination revealed that in spite of his many wounds, Nelson's heart, lungs, kidneys and other organs were all in fine shape, and were like those of a man two decades younger than Nelson's forty-seven years.

From January 4 to 7, 1806, Nelson's body was allowed to lie in state at the Painted Hall of the Greenwich Hospital. About 30,000 people crammed into the space to see him, provoking fears of a macabre riot—at one point, pikes had to be used on the crowds to maintain order. Nelson's fine coffin had been made from wood taken from a French ship, *L'Orient*, which he had captured at the time of his victory on the Nile in 1798. On January 8, his coffin was placed on a barge and sailed westwards up the Thames, and then deposited in the Admiralty—the Royal Navy's headquarters, in Whitehall.

Nelson's lavish funeral

That night was bitterly cold in London, and almost no one was asleep. Parties from all over England had been arriving in the capital over the last few days, the inns and hotels were crammed to bursting and the streets were thronged with those who wanted to ensure a good vantage point along the funeral route.

Finally the sun came up and, after days of overcast weather and fog, it was dazzling. The bells of St. Paul's began to peal at 8:30, by which time almost every mourner was seated at the roadside or hanging out from an upper window. The funeral procession—made up of more than 10,000 troops—was so long that the Scots Greys, who led, had reached the Cathedral before the senior officers who brought up the rear had even left the Admiralty. Later, everyone remarked on a strange noise that filled the air: Though the crowds maintained a respectful silence, the effect of thousands of people doffing their hats in unison sounded like the murmurings of the sea.

By the time the congregation had fully gathered inside St. Paul's, the light was falling, and for a while all was gloom. But then a new chandelier made up of 130 lamps was illuminated, casting its brilliance over the service. The ceremony lasted almost four hours, and at the end of it Nelson's coffin was lowered into the crypt, where it was interred in a large marble sarcophagus, originally commissioned in the sixteenth century by Cardinal Thomas Wolsey, before his fall from favor.

The last part of the funeral was unplanned and unexpected. Surviving crew members of the *Victory* were meant to furl three of their ships flags, riddled with shot-holes, and laid them upon the coffin. Instead, they fell upon the largest flag, tore a great piece from it and divided it up between them, so that each man should have a proper relic of their fallen leader. No one saw anything in the gesture but an expression of love.

It was the grandest funeral any English warrior been granted since that of the poet and soldier Sir Philip Sidney, under Elizabeth. Had Nelson deserved it? To his contemporaries, there was no doubt: He had saved them from invasion by Napoleon, and tyranny. Ten years later, after the victory at Waterloo, it seemed all the more clear that by defeating the French fleet, Nelson had denied Napoleon control of the sea and thus made his defeat by land possible, if not inevitable.

The Funeral of Lord Horatio Nelson in St Paul's Cathedral, by Augustus Charles Pugin, 1806

Under the Victorians, Nelson became revered as the unequaled hero who had brought England a state of peace and prosperity that lasted almost a hundred years, until 1914. And today, a statue of Nelson still stands high above the square named after his most decisive victory, surveying London with a single stone eye.

EMMA, LADY HAMILTON

Life for Nelson's famous mistress began as Amy Lyon in Cheshire in 1765. As a teenager, she worked a series of odd jobs, including as a maid at the Drury Lane Theatre and as a hostess and exotic dancer for the stag party of Sir Harry Featherstonhaugh. It was there that she met Charles Francis Greville. Though she was already pregnant by Sir Harry, she moved to Greville's home, where he took control of her life, changing her name to Emma Hart. Wanting a painting of his beautiful mistress, Greville introduced her to his friend, artist George Romney. She quickly became Romney's muse, posing for over 60 portraits, often in mythological scenes.

As Romney's paintings made her famous, Greville became embarrassed and sent Emma to Naples under the guise of a long vacation—really intending for her to become the mistress of his uncle, Sir William Hamilton, 34 years her elder. Eventually, the pair married, and Lady Hamilton became one of Naples' most famous entertainers. As the wife of the British Envoy, it was Hamilton's job to entertain Nelson when he came to Naples in 1793; the pair met again in 1798, but by then Nelson's appearance had hardened by the years at sea. Still, it was love. The two most famous Britons embarked on a celebrated romance, traveling and living with Lady Hamilton's husband. Emma Hamilton gave birth to a baby girl, Horatia, in 1801.

When Nelson died in 1805, he had asked the state to set aside a pension for Emma and Horatia, but none was given. Emma had lost her youthful allure, and she quickly spent through all the money Hamilton had left her. After a year in debtor's prison, she fled to France, where she died at the age of 49.

CHAPTER 19.

WHEN JOHN KEATS MET FANNY BRAWNE

10 OCTOBER 1819

For several months, John Keats had not seen the young woman whose image tormented him, and he had written to her only once since August 1819. He was anguished by the thought that she had merely been flirting with him in the early, light-hearted days of their romance, back in the spring of that year. Fanny Brawne was, after all, only 19 years old; Keats was 23. And he was still more anguished that she might be, as he put it, a "Cressid," flirtatious with others, perhaps even unfaithful. Over the long summer, away from London, he had poured out his angry jealousy in a series of increasingly frenzied letters, before lapsing into silent suffering.

Despite his short life and relatively slender output, Keats is among the giants of English literature: probably no other poet besides Shakespeare has been so widely read and so profoundly loved. He has always had a special appeal for adolescents, and sensitive young people often make a cult of Keats, not only for his exquisite language and passionate emotions, but because of the seductive tragedy of his early death. Well over a century before James Dean, Keats was the prime example of a sexy genius who burned brightly but all too briefly. He was also, with his longer-lived contemporary William Blake, one of the few major English poets to have been born and raised in

---

John Keats, by William Hilton

London—one reason why the more snobbish critics dismissed him as a "Cockney": an ill-mannered, proletarian Londoner.

John's histrionic outpouring of amorous despair might easily have frightened off an inexperienced young girl, but on Fanny it had the opposite effect. During the time Keats was away from town, she had resolved to devote herself to him entirely. When she opened the door of her home—Wentworth Place, Hampstead—on October 10, 1819, she appeared to him utterly changed; no longer a flighty girl but a mature and loving woman. Keats was more smitten than ever.

Almost at once, he began to write a stream of newly impassioned poems and letters. "I could be Martyred for my Religion," he wrote to her the following day, "Love is my religion—I could die for that—I could die for you. My Creed is Love and you are its only tenet." Seven days after that, he gave her a garnet ring as token of their engagement, though the pact was kept a secret from all but a very few friends. And their living arrangements were a kind of torture. Brawne and her mother lived in one half of Wentworth Place; Keats's friend Charles Brown lived in the other half, separated from the Brawnes by a wall so thin that the inhabitants could hear each other moving around. Keats now became one of those inhabitants.

This was not a wise move, but Keats did not have many other options. He was desperately poor, having already spent most of the small inheritance that had seen him through medical school, and he had long since resolved to give up medicine so as to devote himself to poetry, hardly a more profitable vocation in 1819 than it is today. No wonder Brawne's mother, though she personally liked Keats, thought that he would bring Fanny nothing but misery, and hoped that Fanny's attachment would fade. Keats's attractions were obvious: Though he was very short, barely more than five feet, he had almost girlish good looks, lustrous and well-tended hair and a charming manner. His male friends were as deeply devoted to him as his female admirers. But a mother must be sensible, and Keats did not show much promise as a good provider.

Fanny Brawne

Sexual frustration exacerbated the young man's chronic anxiety and sense of failure. He had not published many poems, and those he had seen into print had been sneered at as ill-bred and embarrassingly sensual. He had recently nursed his brother Tom through a fatal illness and feared that his own sickness—tuberculosis—would prove to be equally deadly. And now here he was, scarcely so much as feet away from the woman he adored, too poor to marry her, too bound by propriety to make love to her, and seething with thwarted desire. It did not help that his housemate, Brown, was much looser in his conduct. Brown had recently employed a young Irish woman, Abigail O'Donaghue, as his housekeeper and promptly seduced her. Keats could hear their energetic couplings, and within mere months Abigail was conspicuously pregnant.

Such tension could not be sustained indefinitely and a crisis came in early February 1820, when Brown discovered Keats coughing blood onto his pillow. Keats asked him to bring a candle, and looked at the color of the stain. "After regarding it steadfastly," Brown wrote that "he looked up in my face, with a calmness of countenance that I can never forget, and said, 'I know the color of that blood; it is arterial blood. I cannot be deceived in that color; that drop of blood is my death warrant; I must die.'"

Very much a child of his age, Keats associated his "consumption"—though he had studied medicine, he never called his illness by any scientific name—with his intense love. (The superstition that consumption was the disease of sensitive poets and ardent lovers lasted well into the twentieth century.) Barely fifty years earlier, when almost every author had aspired to the classical virtues of decorum, emotional restraint, civility and sobriety, the work of Keats would have seemed like the outpourings of a maniac. His poetry could be wild, ardent and even morbid—he dwells not only on

Left: *John Keats at Wentworth Place*, by Joseph Severn, 1821; Right: Keats' House at Hampstead Heath

death in the abstract but in rotting corpses and grave-worms. But the first generation of Romantics (as we now call them), Samuel Taylor Coleridge and William Wordsworth, had changed all the rules. They focussed more on the self than on society, more on the country than the town, more on mysticism than on reason, more on expressiveness than politeness. Keats's poetry was not quite in their vein—for one thing, it was much more erotic—but the older writers had made it possible for him to write in his idiosyncratic voice. Not many people had heard of Keats, but some of those who did had recognized his genius at once.

The more ill he became, the more powerful his obsession with Fanny grew. In his mind, the woman he worshipped was also the force that was killing him. Eventually, his friends decided that the only thing that might save Keats was to take him to live in the health-giving climate of Rome, with his crony, the painter Joseph Severn. Keats left for Italy on September 13, 1820. Both he and Fanny Brawne took care to make their parting unemotional. They had agreed that when (or if) he returned from Rome, they would marry and set up house with her family. It was not to be. Keats died on February 23, 1821. Hardly anyone outside his small, devoted set of friends noted the fact. One of his friends, Percy Shelley, wrote an elegy for Keats, "Adonais," a poem which would form the basis of the Keatsian legend of doomed, youthful genius that began to spring up later in the nineteenth century and has not waned to this day.

John Keats was just twenty-five years and four months old when he died. He had only begun writing poems in the last six years. It is astonishing that such a career should have yielded so many masterpieces, including a handful of odes that are among the most perfect in the English language. It is still more astonishing that the majority of his most enduring works were composed in a single year from late 1818 to late 1819, months in which he was ill, constantly short of money and hopelessly in love with a woman he could not and would not ever have.

Left: *Portrait of Keats on His Death Bed, From a Drawing,* by Joseph Severn, reproduced 1895

Fanny Brawne remained in her mourning clothes for more than three years. In 1833 she finally married, and bore her husband, Louis Lindo, two children. She died in 1865. By her own account, she never took off the ring that Keats had given her.

CHAPTER 20.

THE YOUNG DICKENS IS SENT TO WORK IN A BLACKING FACTORY

1824

For a delicate boy, it was hell. After a comfortable, even idyllic childhood, Charles Dickens was suddenly, at the age of twelve, yanked out of school and sent to labor in a factory—a manufacturer of shoe polish. Warren's Blacking Factory, it was called, near the Thames on Hungerford Stairs, close by the present-day Charing Cross Station. For ten hours a day, Charles had to paste labels onto bottles of boot-blacking, while his fellow workers jeered at him and bullied him for his delicate ways. (One of them was called Fagin. He would remember that name.) Worse than the toil and the insults was the fact that his workstation was right next to a window, so that all the passersby could stare in at him as he labored; he had never known such humiliation.

Horrible as his working day was, the hours before and after were worse. In 1824, London still had no proper police force: that would come five years later, with Sir Robert Peel's foundation of the Metropolitan Police. The city was growing more and more prosperous, and by the end of Dickens's life in 1870 was the richest capital in the world, but there was a vast army of dispossessed Londoners who had no part in that wealth unless they stole it. Just feet away from wealthy, ornate parades like the Strand were narrow streets and alleyways that teemed with the homeless, the desperate and the

Dickens at the Blacking Warehouse, by Fred Bernard, 1904

dangerous. Charles had to scurry through these mean streets all alone, buying his own scraps of food and running from the street people who took an ominous interest in him. At night he went back to his filthy room on the other side of the Thames, in the district known as Borough. He felt alone and abandoned, as he recalled in a private autobiographical sketch he wrote two decades later: "No words can express the secret agony of my soul…My whole nature was so penetrated with the grief and humiliation of [the experience] that even now, famous and caressed and happy, I often forget in my dreams that I have a dear wife and children; even that I am a man; and wander desolately back to that time of my life."

He had no way of knowing it at the time, but this period of industrial servitude would only last for five months. It might easily have gone on for years, or until the boy found less honest toil: "But for the mercy of God, I might easily have been, for all the care that was taken of me, a little robber or a little vagabond." The cause of Dickens's sufferings was his father's reckless way with money. John Dickens had worked for the Navy Pay Office, first in Portsmouth and then, after a brief London interlude, in Chatham, a naval town in Kent. The five years the Dickens family spent here were happy ones for the future novelist. But his father lived well beyond his modest salary—it did not help that he had sired seven children—and when he was posted back to London, he decided that the cost of Charles's education was not worth it. Like countless debtors before him, John Dickens was locked up in the Marshalsea Prison, which had stood in Southwark since the fourteenth century.

His wife and some of his children joined him there, and by most accounts their conditions were reasonably comfortable. The prison was, in effect, an extortion racket. If you had a little money to give the jailors, you could enjoy such luxuries as a shop, a restaurant and a bar, and could even be let out by day. If you were penniless, you would be crammed into a cell with dozens of strangers and count yourself lucky to be given a little bread and water. Poorer prisoners simply starved to death; at one time, the authorities noted that about 300 had died of hunger in the space of three months.

The Dickens family crisis was resolved by a timely inheritance of 450 pounds from John's mother, Elizabeth

The condition of London's poor in the 19th century

Dickens, and by the passing of the Insolvent Debtors' Act, which made life much easier for those with credit problems. In principle, Charles could have been taken away from the factory at once, but he stayed on for a few more weeks because his mother was keen for him to carry on earning a living. Charles was horrified: "I do not write resentfully or angrily, for I know that all these things have worked together to make me what I am. But I never afterwards forgot, I never shall forget, I never can forget that my mother was warm for my being sent back." His father took a more kindly view, and Charles was sent back to school for another three years.

Charles's rise to fame was fairly swift. On leaving school in 1827, he worked as a junior clerk in some law offices. He learned shorthand and launched himself as a journalist, first reporting on legal matters and then on Parliamentary debates. He thrived at the writing trade — *David Copperfield* tells the tale — and in his few spare hours he began to write humorous sketches. In 1836, he began to serialize his first major work, *Pickwick*

Dickens's beloved home in Kent, Gad's Hill Place, 1856

Papers. Readers found it hilarious, and his fame rocketed. Two decades later, in 1856, he was more than wealthy enough to buy a grand country house—Gad's Hill Place, in Higham, Kent. When Charles was a little boy, his father had pointed to this very mansion on one of their walks and told his son that, if he worked hard enough, he might be able to own it. So one childhood dream came true. It did not make him happy.

Compared to some forms of childhood suffering, five months in a blacking factory might seem like a relatively mild trauma. But Dickens was an almost pathologically sensitive child, who felt both pains and pleasures deeply, and most of the people who have written about him believe that he was right to say that his miseries in the factory helped make him the novelist he eventually became.

His novels teem with lonely, abandoned, helpless children, who are usually orphans, paupers or invalids—Oliver Twist; Little Nell in *The Old Curiosity Shop*; the semi-autobiographical hero of *David Copperfield*; Paul Dombey in *Dombey and Son*; Pip in *Great Expectations*; Jo the crossing-sweeper in *Bleak House*—and the sense of the world as a nightmarish, absurd place where a child or adult may be arbitrarily doomed or just as arbitrarily rescued is also a legacy of that childhood penance. (Dostoyevsky loved

Dickens's novels and learned from them; so did Kafka.) This is the night side of Dickens's sensibility—the side that is always lurking like a feral beast outside the loving, merry households where the table groans with food, aged relatives are kindly and twinkling, handsome young lovers court simpering young ladies and children frolic underfoot. If Dickens had truly been no more than a cheerleader for Victorian domesticity, he would have been long forgotten.

But his twelve-year-old soul had been seared with terror and rage and loneliness. The recognition that countless other children had suffered far worse, and were still suffering, made him an ardent social crusader, both in his fiction and as an active philanthropist. It has been said that Dickens was in many ways a conservative—he was a keen supporter of the British Empire, and for all his wide-reaching compassion was known to complain that prisoners had too easy a time these days. And yet his searing accounts of the conditions of the outcast, the corruption of the law, the venality and incompetence of politicians, and the insufferable, smug hypocrisy of the new moneyed classes were as furious as anything to be found in Marx or Engels. And unlike that glum duo, Dickens was read by the very people he was mocking and flaying—and they loved him. He was by far the most financially successful novelist of his day, and his works have never been out of print. It was never enough. Always inside him was that twelve-year-old boy, humiliated, frightened, and utterly alone.

CHAPTER 21.

THE WEDDING OF QUEEN VICTORIA AND ALBERT
10 FEBRUARY 1840

The bridegroom was only twenty. So was the bride; but, despite her youth, she had already been Queen of England for two years. Victoria was wearing a white satin dress with a sapphire brooch set with diamonds—a present from her husband-to-be, Albert. On her head was a wreath of orange flower blossoms, which, as the congregation could all see, quivered a great deal. She was nervous. Albert, dressed in the uniform of a British field marshal, looked nervous too, and very pale. Victoria's progress up the aisle of the Chapel Royal in St. James's Palace was a little awkward, since her train was too short to be held properly by all the bridesmaids, who had to tiptoe forwards so as not to tread on each other's ankles. No matter. Victoria may have been nervous, but she was intensely happy.

So familiar is the grim, brooding face of the old Victoria that it is hard to remember that she came to the throne as a young girl, and a lively young girl at that. Her childhood had been lonely, and her home in Kensington Palace lacked any of the usual comforts: "I never had a room to myself, I never had a sofa and there was not a single carpet that was not threadbare." (The dwellings of the English aristocracy, when not being used for grand displays of wealth, have long been notorious for their shabbiness and discomfort.

Queen Victoria

New, comfortable furniture was the giveaway sign of recent wealth.) Victoria spent her days either all alone with her beloved dolls, or in the company of men and women of late middle age. But as soon as she was old enough, she threw herself into social pleasures with enormous gusto. She adored dancing, and would often be the very last to leave a ball at two or three. She loved her little dog, Dash, and her horses, which she would ride at dangerous speed.

She was also very young for her years, particularly when it came to men. Before marriage, her closest male companion had been her advisor Viscount Melbourne (the Whig Prime Minister from 1835 until 1841), who was 58 when she was crowned. She found him kind, delightfully funny and wise, and she trusted him as she had rarely trusted anyone. It helped that he was a skilled flatterer, but his flattery was not insincere. One witness noted "when [Melbourne] is with her he looks loving, contented, a little pleased with himself; respectful, at his ease, as if accustomed to take first place in the circle, and dreamy and gay—all mixed up together." In short, they were enjoying a Platonic love affair, though she would have been shocked to hear that people were saying that her feelings were "*sexual* though she [did] not know it."

Sooner or later, though, a Queen has to marry—and, at this date, marry into royalty. After ruling out half a dozen or so unmarried royals from France, Prussia, Denmark, Schleswig-Holstein and elsewhere, the most likely candidate proved to be a distant German cousin, Prince Albert, Duke of Saxe-Coburg and Gotha. Albert was said to have been a beautiful child, shy and sensitive to the point of effeminacy. As an adult, he was stiff in his manners with men and terrified of women. Victoria and Albert had first met when they were sixteen. She was somewhat taken aback by his sickliness and inability to stay up late, but pleased by his looks and his gentleness. He was much less keen on her, describing her merely as "amiable," hardly the most impassioned of adjectives.

Victoria was reluctant to marry young; she was enjoying her new freedoms far too much to wish a different kind of restriction in her life. And Melbourne, who did not greatly admire the Saxe-Coburgs in particular or the Germans in general, thought Albert a poor prospect

William Lamb, 2nd Viscount Melbourne, by Sir Edwin Henry Landseer, 1836

as a royal spouse. Soon, Victoria was beginning to speak of marriage as "odious," and said that she "dreaded the thought of getting married." But her tune changed the next time Albert came to visit.

At half past seven on the evening of October 10, 1839, Victoria stood at the top of the main stairs in Windsor Castle to greet her German guests, who had been delayed by bad weather in the English channel and had all suffered quite badly from sea-sickness. In spite of Albert's drained appearance, she experienced that rare thing, an instant surge of love. Albert, she said, was "beautiful" in every point: his figure, his "fine waist," his "delicate" moustache, his "exquisite" nose...her heart began to pound immoderately.

Five days later, she proposed to him. (Royal protocol dictates that queens must do the asking.) He accepted with apparent gladness, and everyone noted that Victoria was now ecstatic with happiness. Nor was she quite as detached from her instincts as she had been in the days when Melbourne was her favorite. When Albert accompanied her to review troops in Hyde Park, she was thrilled to note that he wore a pair of white cashmere trousers with "*nothing under them.*" And though Albert had been accused of effeminacy when younger, he was certainly virile enough as Prince Consort. Within four weeks of their honeymoon, Victoria was known to be pregnant.

Family of Queen Victoria, by Franz Xavier Winterhalter, 1846

Over the next twenty years, until his death from typhoid at the age of forty-two—Victoria was devastated—Victoria bore him another eight children. The couple would bicker occasionally, but most of the time they were very happy. Their marriage set a pattern for the nation—certainly for the rising middle classes, but also in some measure for the aristocracy, who had previously tended to drunkenness, rowdyism, sexual license and brutality. The strange popular image of the English as quietly spoken, emotionally reserved, law-abiding and hypocritical about sex is largely a legacy of Victoria and Albert. Victoria was not a woman with the vast intellectual gifts and political cunning of, say, Elizabeth I; and yet under her long reign, England became, for several decades, the world's leading nation.

By 1870, the value of Britain's overseas exports had reached the then-staggering total of twenty million pounds per year—more than four times that of the United States, and more than the total output of France, Germany and Italy combined. Britain had the largest navy in the world, and the largest merchant navy, too—more than 20,000 commercial vessels. Both of them protected and reaped the fruits of the world's largest empire. But Victorian Britain had other things to boast of besides great wealth. The development of Robert Peel's police force made London, and then the nation as a whole, far safer than it had ever been. Slowly but perceptibly, the conditions of the poor, and of women and children, improved as a result of enlightened legislation. Science flourished—this was the age of Darwin and of Faraday—as did engineering, and literature (Dickens, George Eliot, Tennyson, Browning, Arnold, Ruskin) and the arts (Turner, the Pre-Raphaelites).

Victoria's reign can be summed up by one word: "progress." The underlying cause of all this near-miraculous national success was simply that England was the first country in the world to make the rapid transformation from an agrarian to an industrial economy. But when people are, on the whole, happy with their daily lives, they are happy with their rulers. Victoria's relationship with her people had violent ups and downs—especially in the early years of her widowhood, when she gave herself over almost entirely to mourning—by the end of her reign, some 60 years after her joyful wedding day, she was sincerely loved by millions.

CHAPTER 22

THE OPENING OF THE FLORENCE NIGHTINGALE SCHOOL OF NURSING

24 JUNE 1860

She was just forty years old, but was internationally celebrated; almost as famous, in fact, as her own Queen, and in many circles more profoundly admired. Florence Nightingale's most fabled exploit, as the "Lady of the Lamp" who traveled independently to Crimea in 1854 to nurse wounded British soldiers, had made her a figure of myth—virtually a modern saint. What had driven her there? Her contemporaries did not often ask that question, and it was not until the publication of Lytton Strachey's essay on her in his iconoclastic 1918 book *Eminent Victorians* that it became socially acceptable to discuss her as anything other than the modest, delicate maiden of high degree who cast aside easy living to tender to the afflicted. The motivations of the real Nightingale, Strachey argued, were much more interesting: "A Demon possessed her."

There are several ways of trying to understand her hard and complex character and one of the best can be found by studying her proto-feminist tract *Cassandra*, which was not published until 1928, long after her death. (It was not widely read, but it has been described by a leading American critic as the most important work of English feminism between Mary Woolstonecraft and Virginia Woolf.) She had begun the book in 1852 and developed it into a polemic of ferocious intensity. One of her principal charges against contemporary Britain was that it condemned girls and women of the well-to-do classes, women like herself, to lives of unremitting triviality. "Is man's time more valuable than woman's," she asks, "or is the difference between man and woman this, that woman has confessedly nothing to do?" For Florence, finding something to do was a kind of personal revolution. She was seriously ill for much of her life, and it now seems to us as if she may have been using her illness as a way to escape the horrific day-by-day boredom of polite women's lives.

To her parent's dismay, she also refused again and again to accept proposals of marriage, no matter how rich or noble her suitors. After several anguished years, she finally found a way both out of her suffocating family and her chronic illness by tending to the illnesses of two family members, her grandmother and her childhood nurse. It was a revelation for her: She would cure herself by curing others. In the face of intense disapproval from her family, she set about training herself to be not just a nurse, but the best nurse in the world. This skill, combined with her iron resolve, persuaded the Minister of War to send her off to aid British soldiers in the Crimea.

By the time of her return from the Crimean War in 1856, Nightingale was already a living legend; admirers mobbed her in the streets. She immediately set about lobbying for a series of reforms in health care, both for the British Army and in the civilian world. Important public figures rushed to join her, and donations flooded in from an adoring public. By 1859, she had more than 45,000 pounds at her disposal. She decided that one of the things her country most urgently needed was a secular school of nursing; up to this point, the training of nurses throughout Europe had been a matter for churches and monastic orders. On July 9, 1860, the Florence Nightingale School opened as part of the ancient hospital of St. Thomas, in Southwark.

This was an event of huge significance, both for Nightingale and for the world. Together with the publication of her best-selling book *Notes on Nursing* the year earlier, the opening of this school marked the beginning of modern nursing. Before Nightingale, it had generally been assumed that a nurse would be an ill-educated, probably filthy, possibly alcoholic old crone, like Dickens's boozy Mrs. Gamp. The idea that nursing might be a profession seemed almost as far-fetched as the idea that babysitting or

The Sick and Injured in Balaklava at Crimean War, by William Simpson

begging might as well. There was not much in *Notes on Nursing* that would strike us as less than good common sense, but there had never been such a book before—a slim, 136 page volume that tore into bad nursing practice with angry glee, and brought together all the best principles for healthcare known to the age. She may not have properly understood the nature of germs, but she knew that good sanitation was essential to care and cure.

Her influence spread around the world at wildfire speed. During the American Civil War, the leaders of the Union called on her for official advice, while volunteer nurses in field hospitals carried her book with them. To this day, recruits to the profession in many lands still swear a Nightingale oath. But it would have taken a wild optimist to have guessed all this in 1860, when her school would have seemed a fragile and ill-fated thing.

When the first fifteen probationers showed up two weeks later, on July 9, in their brown dresses and white caps and aprons, they found themselves crowded into small, comfortless cubicles in one of St. Thomas's wings. Two years later, thanks to a complicated wrangle about where and how the

Nightingale Receiving the Wounded at Scutari, by Jerry Barrett

hospital should be re-located, they were all shunted off to a temporary home in a former zoo in Newington, where the one-time Giraffe House was the cholera ward and the Elephant House was used for dissections. It was not until more than ten years later, on June 21, 1871, that Queen Victoria opened the new St. Thomas's Hospital on a site immediately opposite the Houses of Parliament on the south bank of the Thames. The Florence Nightingale School finally had a proper home—and in a rather magnificent building, though its magnificence came to an end in the Second World War when it took a direct bomb hit. Today, the School houses the Nightingale Museum.

Florence Nightingale's reputation went into a decline in the first part of the twentieth century. People became uneasily aware that her efforts in the Crimea, while indisputably heroic, were also ill-judged, since she was unaware of the role played in the transmission of disease by germs. (As late as 1911, it was reported that she had cut the fatality rate among injured troops from 42 percent to 2 percent. The grim fact is that mortality rates actually went up during her time in the Crimea.) But over the last couple of decades, she has come to seem not only a more complex figure than the ministering angel of Victorian folklore but a more heroic one.

Modern historians have become frank about the horrors of events that used to be veiled in polite evasions. We now know that the conditions of the men Nurse Nightingale treated were disgusting—so much so that most doctors were refusing even to enter the wards, let alone treat patients. The hospital in which she worked was flooded with human feces. All the latrines were blocked; there were twenty chamber pots to a thousand men, and almost everyone had diarrhea. There was next to no ventilation and the temperatures were unendurably hot. One clergyman, bending down to listen to a soldier's dying words, found his Bible overrun with lice. No one was safe, and Florence herself came down with dysentery, fever and other conditions. But she remained resolute; except at the height of her fevers, she worked on.

Small wonder that, after she came back to England, Nightingale remained an invalid for much of the rest of her life, and spent the better part of the next six years in bed—working prodigiously at writing and reading, but nonetheless in bed. She suffered from all her familiar ailments: headaches, insomnia, palpitations and above all, severe breathing difficulties, now compounded by a sense of failure and worthlessness. Some modern doctors have suggested that she may have been suffering from a condition known as brucellosis, usually caused by eating contaminated meat or drinking contaminated milk; others have thought that all her ills were really psychological.

Invalid or hypochondriac, she was a woman of amazing talent and resolve. She was a brilliant statistician, who helped popularize the use of pie charts. Her quirks are as fascinating as her virtues. Nightingale liked to compare herself to another nocturnal bird, the owl, and used to keep a small owl, Athena, as her pet. (She also kept flocks of cats.) Later, she developed the habit of calling herself a "vampyre," in remorse for the way she drove her workers and supporters so hard that they ended up drained, or actually died from overwork. In her seventies, she finally grew a little plumper, and seemed a little happier. It was the start of her senility. She retreated into her bedroom in her house near Hyde Park in 1896 and remained there for the next fourteen years, until her death in 1910. Her myth endures.

CHAPTER 23.

THE MURDER OF
MARY JANE KELLY
9 NOVEMBER 1888

Dorset Street, Spitalfields, was long called "the worst street in London." It was about to live up to its name with a vengeance.

At about 10:45 in the morning of November 9, 1888, a debt collector named Thomas Bowyer walked down Dorset Street, turned into a shabby, decaying tenement called Miller's Court and banged at the door of No. 13. A prostitute named Mary Jane Kelly lived there, which wasn't unusual, as there were hundreds, maybe thousands, of prostitutes living and working in the East End slums. Bowyer had come to claim money from her. She owed her landlord six weeks' rent: twenty-nine shillings. There was no response, so he banged and banged with his fist before deciding on another tactic. He found a broken window that was stuffed with an old coat, pulled the scruffy garment aside and peered into the gloom. It must have taken him a second or so to adjust to the darkness. Then he must have screamed, or vomited, or both. Anyone would have.

The body was so hideously mutilated that it was scarcely recognizable as female, or even human. A couple of hours later, the Metropolitan Police arrived with a pair of doctors. The medical men made a methodical study of poor Mary's remains, noted in full, dispassionate detail. It is hard to read this document without a shudder: To dilute the horror a little, let's just say that her throat had been slit as deep as the vertebrae, her face mutilated with severe gashes from a large knife and most of her inner organs were removed. Her uterus, her kidneys, her breasts, her liver, her intestines and her spleen had all been taken out, and they were placed with apparent care on the bed and around the room. Her heart was completely missing. They estimated that it must have taken the killer at least two hours to carry out this strenuous dissection. Mary's shabby room was poorly furnished, but the police did notice one strange detail: a cheap kettle, from which the spout had just been melted free. Clearly, the murderer had made an intensely hot blaze in the fireplace, probably fed by the victim's clothes.

London's press fell on the story at once and had no hesitation in identifying Mary Jane Kelly as the fifth and latest victim of "Jack the Ripper," even though Mary was, at about twenty-five, a good fifteen years younger than the four previous victims, and the extent of her mutilation greatly exceeded that of the other murders. Posterity now identifies her as the last of the five so-called "canonical" Ripper victims, though almost nothing about the nature of the Ripper can be stated with much certainty. Prostitutes were murdered all the time in East London, and especially in the "worst street," where violent death was almost a weekly event. Between April 3, 1888, and February 13, 1891, there were at least eleven cases of prostitutes being killed; these were referred to collectively as the Whitechapel murders. Only five show the signature marks of the Ripper's modus operandi—facial mutilation, deep slashes to the throat, partial or complete destruction of the abdominal or genital areas and removal of inner organs. As far as we know, the Ripper abandoned his mission after Mary Jane Kelly. But on November 9, 1888, no one knew that this mysterious killing spree would be over; the city was in a state of utter fear.

The nightmare had begun just over two months earlier, on August 31, when Mary Ann Nichols was killed on Duck's Row. About a week later, on September 8, Annie Chapman met her end on Hanbury Street, Spitalfields. Then, on September 30 came two deaths on one night: Elizabeth Stride in Dutfield's Yard, and Catherine Eddowes in Mitre Square. This was an age when sensationalist popular newspapers were coming into their own, and the press helped fan the flames of terror and paranoia. Crank letters flooded in, some denouncing Irish or Jewish immigrants in the East End as the likely

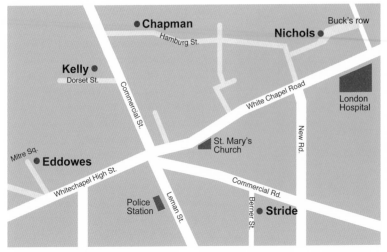

Locations of the Whitechapel murders

culprits, others advancing theories as to who the killer might be. For a while, the shadowy man was known as "Leather Apron," since, it was argued, only a butcher or a slaughterhouse laborer could have the strength and anatomical knowledge to carry out these mutilations. Then came the letters signed "Saucy Jack," or "Jack the Ripper," and the hideous facts of the case began to mutate into durable legend.

There are many reasons why the Ripper murders gripped the contemporary imagination and continue to fascinate some people more than 120 years later. The simplest one is that they remain unsolved, and people love to fill in the crossword of mystery with their own ingenious contrivances. Another is that they combine horror with intimacy. A death toll of just five is almost infinitesimal compared to the genocides and massacres of the twentieth century, but atrocity on a grand scale numbs the imagination. The scary thing about Jack, like other bogeymen, is that he comes creeping out of the darkness to kill a single person; in our nightmares, to kill us. And then there is the sense that the Ripper was a monster created by the cruel social conditions of the time, a monster from the sleep of reason.

London in the 1880s was a city more spectacularly divided between wealth and poverty than it had ever been. There had always been rich districts and

THE NEMESIS OF NEGLECT.

"THERE FLOATS A PHANTOM OF THE SLUM'S FOUL AIR, SHAPING, TO EYES WHICH HAVE THE GIFT OF SEEING, INTO THE SPECTRE OF THAT LOATHLY LAIR. FACE IT—FOR VAIN IS FLEEING! RED-HANDED, RUTHLESS, FURTIVE, UNERECT, 'TIS MURDEROUS CRIME—THE NEMESIS OF NEGLECT."

The Nemesis of Neglect, by John Tenniel, 1888

poor districts, but the richer parts of the nation's capital—also the capital of a vast and profitable empire—were rich to a degree that had never been seen before. The West End, which is still London's main playground in the twenty-first century, was where that prodigious wealth was most visible. Here—around Piccadilly, Mayfair, St. James's, Belgravia and the Strand—were grand houses, gentlemen's clubs, ornate theatres and opera houses, sumptuous restaurants, huge department stores and small, exclusive retailers selling luxury goods imported from all across the globe. It was the haunt of gentlemen and ladies of fashion and of means, who shopped and danced and ate prodigious quantities of food: A prosperous Englishman of the day would consume something like four times as many calories as his present-day counterpart, at meals which ran to well over a dozen courses, well lubricated with assorted wines and spirits. And barely a few miles away, in the East End, life was a hell of violence, hunger, poor sanitation, overcrowded tenements, disease and premature death. Humanitarian attempts to improve life there had not made much difference, and there were streets which the police would refuse to enter unless in groups. Those politicians and writers who bothered about such things sensed that some kind of violent catastrophe was waiting in the wings.

The popular comic magazine *Punch*, usually given to feeble jokes about clergymen and maiden aunts, caught this idea brilliantly in a famous cartoon, "The Nemesis of Neglect," which shows a knife-wielding ghoul rising from the slums. London had treated its poor like subhuman beasts, and now the beasts were coming to get London. The sense of guilt and menace even affected the gaiety of the West End, where a play based on *Dr. Jekyll and Mr. Hyde* had been a major hit of that year. On the show's last night, the lead actor (who was himself accused of the murders by imaginative writers) addressed the audience and explained why the show was being taken off: "Ladies and Gentlemen, there are horrors enough outside here."

WHO WAS JACK THE RIPPER?

The identity of Jack the Ripper has eluded investigators for over a century. Between 1888 and 1891, over 2,000 people were interviewed by authorities, upwards of 300 were investigated and 80 were detained. The list of suspects is now well over one hundred names and includes eyebrow-raisers like *Alice in Wonderland* author Lewis Carroll and *Jekyll and Hide* actor Richard Mansfield.

Puck magazine, featuring cartoonist Tom Merry's depiction of Jack the Ripper

Despite the lack of hard evidence, the Chief Constable of the London Metropolitan Police, Melville Macnaghten, named three suspects in an 1894 memorandum: Kosminski (last name only), Montague Druitt and Michael Ostrog. The Kosminski in question was Aaron, a poor Polish Jewish immigrant who suffered from dementia and paranoia and was institutionalized in 1891. An interesting twist in the Kosminski tale, a David Cohen (the Jewish equivalent of a John Doe)–who exhibited violent and antisocial behavior after being incarcerated in 1888–was named Nathan Kaminski, making it probable that investigators confused the name. An FBI profiler later wrote that behavioral clues gathered from the murders all point to a person "known to the police as David Cohen...or someone very much like him." The other two leads are even weaker. Druitt, a 31-year-old barrister who did not reside in Whitechapel, was suspected because of his suicide by drowning in 1888. Ostrog was imprisoned in France during the Ripper murders.

There is also a Masonic/royal conspiracy theory at the center of the murders, which formed the basis of a BBC show and subsequent "tell-all" book. In these accounts, Queen Victoria's physician, Sir William Withey Gull, is the Ripper. Gull and an accomplice murdered the women because the prostitutes knew of an illegitimate child that the Queen's grandson, Prince Albert Victor (Eddy), had with a poor Catholic girl. To deflect attention, Montague Druitt was blamed and his suicide was staged.

Why had the Prince frequented one of the city's most dangerous and impoverished neighborhoods? He took lessons from local painter Walter Sickert, who, the legend goes, painted telling clues in his works. Lack of strong evidence, and the fact that any witnesses are long dead, leave this terrifying mystery with no clear culprit.

CHAPTER 24

THE DINNER THAT LAUNCHED SHERLOCK HOLMES

10 AUGUST 1889

It was surely one of the most productive meals in the history of literature. An American editor, Joseph Marshall Stoddart, had come to London to sign up promising writers for *Lippincott's Magazine* of Philadelphia. Following tips from his associates, he invited a handful of rising talents to a dinner in the sumptuous surroundings of the Langham Hotel. One was a large Irishman, flamboyantly dressed, a loud and brilliant talker: Oscar Wilde. Another was a bluff, cheerful Scottish medical man, dressed in no-nonsense tweeds and with a ruddy outdoors complexion: Dr. Arthur Conan Doyle. By the end of the evening, Stoddart had signed both of them up for a hundred pounds each, to produce fictions of some 40,000 words. Wilde duly wrote *The Picture of Dorian Gray*. Conan Doyle wrote *The Sign of Four*, a ripping yarn about a detective called Sherlock Holmes.

This was the second Holmes story: the first, "A Study in Scarlet" had appeared in *Beeton's Christmas Annual* for 1887. Conan Doyle had found it difficult to place the story, which he had written at great speed in March and April of 1886, but when it was finally sold, for just twenty-five pounds, and had been published, it met with a fairly warm reception from the public. Even so, the author had a hunch that there might be an audience for more

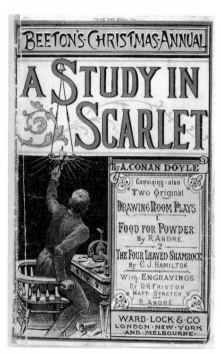

Beeton's Christmas Annual, 1887, featuring Arthur Conan Doyle's "A Study in Scarlet."

Holmes tales. He was diffident about some aspects of his new novella, though, and wrote ruefully to Stoddart: "It must amuse you to see the vast and accurate knowledge of London which I display. I worked it all out from a Post Office map." The fact was that Doyle, a native of Edinburgh and now a resident of a small town on the south coast of England, had only ever paid a few brief visits to London. How curious that he should be the city's most potent mythologist since Dickens.

The Sign of Four was published by Stoddart in February 1890 to great enthusiasm: Holmes became famous in America a good year and a half before the cult of the Great Detective took off in London. By that time, Conan Doyle was a proper Londoner himself, living in a fine house in Bloomsbury and renting a consulting room for his ophthalmology practice at 2, Upper Wimpole Street. But there was no business for him. "I waited in the consulting room and no-one waited in the waiting room." Profoundly bored, he finished his historical novel *The White Company* and began thinking about how he might boost his income.

The answer, he believed, was original to him. (This was not entirely true.) In the Victorian period, most fiction was first published in magazines, and in serial form. Conan Doyle saw a weakness here; if a reader were to miss an installment or two of a novel, however good, she or he might well lose interest and stop buying the magazine. Instead of a serial he proposed the simple idea of a series, in which the same characters would appear again and again, but each episode would be a self-contained short story. "To test this theory," as he put it, he wrote two more tales about Holmes: "A Scandal in Bohemia" and "The Red-Headed League," and he sold them to the recently founded *Strand* magazine for a healthy sum.

Left: Walter Paget; Right: *Sherlock Holmes*, by Sidney Paget, 1904

"A Scandal in Bohemia" first appeared in the *Strand* in July 1891, illustrated by a little-known commercial artist, Sidney Paget. The story goes that a letter commissioning a portrait of the detective had actually been addressed to Sidney's better-known brother, Walter Paget, who was also an illustrator. Whether or not this is true, Walter was happy to pose for his brother, with the result that the image of Holmes was much more handsome than the skinny bohemian described by Conan Doyle.

"A Scandal in Bohemia" was a hit, and the beginning of Holmes mania. When the second of the *Strand* tales appeared in the August issue, people queued up from dawn outside newsagents' stores to demand their copies. The *Strand's* circulation jumped by 100,000 copies per issue every time a Holmes story was announced on the cover. When the first set of stories was re-issued in book form in October 1892, the volume was an immediate bestseller, and within three years had been bought by a quarter of a million delighted fans.

Why was Holmes such a hit? Partly, it was a matter of sheer novelty. Apart from three short stories by Edgar Allan Poe, about the almost supernaturally brilliant poet-logician C. Auguste Dupin, there had hardly been any yarns of criminal detection in English-language fiction. (French fiction was a different matter.) The success of Conan Doyle's creation opened the floodgates, so that nowadays bookstores, movie theaters and television

"HOLMES PULLED OUT HIS WATCH."

Sherlock Holmes (r) and Dr. John H. Watson in *The Greek Interpreter*, by Sidney Paget, 1893

screens are crammed with latter-day versions of Sherlock—sometimes, indeed, with the man himself. Then as now, audiences loved seeing the way in which Mr. Holmes could encounter an apparently insoluble problem and take it apart with effortless ease. They also enjoyed Holmes's eccentricities—his violin-playing, his cocaine habit, his fits of indolence—as well as his apparent indifference to normal human weaknesses, including love. And they relished the wonderful chemistry between the bizarre genius and his devoted friend and serial biographer, Dr. John Watson: the ordinary, decent fellow who served as the reader's representative in the Holmes universe.

Conan Doyle was understandably pleased by all the money his creation was bringing in, but irked that these fables of detection were drawing attention away from his other literary works, at which he worked far more diligently and whose quality he considered far superior. Before 1891 was out, he was already musing that Holmes "has got to be an 'old man of the sea' about my neck, and I intend to make an end of him. If I don't he will make an end of me." An entry in his workbook for 1893 reads simply: "Kill Holmes." Soon, horrified readers would groan at the prospect of Holmes plummeting to his death at the Reichenbach Falls, locked in a vicious embrace with Professor Moriarty, the "Napoleon of Crime." Twenty thousand *Strand* readers cancelled their subscriptions.

For years, Conan Doyle remained stubborn in his refusal to bring Holmes back from his watery grave. But Holmes was a hard man to keep down for long, and by the end of the century he had crept back as the leading character in a long story originally intended simply as a flesh-creeper about a ghostly dog, "The Hound of the Baskervilles." It was published in August 1901, and once again audiences went wild. An American periodical, *Collier's Weekly,* offered Conan Doyle the dazzling sum of 45,000 dollars for 15 more Sherlock stories, and he reluctantly agreed. Holmes was with him to stay, and the author and his creation would not finally part company until 1927. By that time, Conan Doyle was Sir Arthur, and the richest writer in the world.

Arthur Conan Doyle, 1893

And what about Holmes? As Orson Welles once put it, the detective was probably the most famous man who never existed. And certainly the most famous Londoner who never lived.

CHAPTER 25.

THE TRIALS OF
OSCAR WILDE
14 FEBRUARY TO 22 MAY, 1895

Had there ever been a fall from grace so sudden, so profound?

The freezing cold evening of St. Valentine's Day, 1895, marked the greatest triumph of Oscar Wilde's life. His latest play, *The Importance of Being Earnest*, opened at the St. James's Theatre, Duke Street, and was immediately acknowledged as his comic masterpiece: a rapturously funny work that savaged conventional values with such wit, ingenuity and elegance that all but the sternest souls were enchanted. It was a success without equal on the London stage. One distinguished man of the theater said that he had not seen such an ecstatic reception for a new play in more than fifty years. Wilde, floridly dressed for the occasion and sporting his trademark green carnation, had every reason to feel like a conquering hero.

Though he had only begun to write his famous comedies three years earlier, Wilde was now, at forty, a giant of the West End, fully the equal of George Bernard Shaw—who was just about the only critic to give the play a poor review. Wilde's previous comedy, *An Ideal Husband*, was still a major hit.. News of Oscar's wonderful coup soon reached as far as the United States, where the *New York Times* declared, "Oscar Wilde may be said to have at last, and by a single stroke, put his enemies under his feet."

How wrong that reporter was. Wilde's deadliest enemy, John Sholto Douglas, ninth Marquess of Queensberry, had been prevented by the theater management from staging a demonstration on the opening night, but his next attack was imminent. Queensberry had been intent on destroying Wilde since 1892, when Oscar fell in love with the gentleman's youthful son, Alfred Douglas, known to his friends as "Bosie."

Wilde and Lord Alfred Douglas, 1893

In Queensberry's eyes, Wilde was the satanic corrupter of his son, though the record suggests that Bosie—a poet and author known in London for his vanity and extravagant ways—was the one who led Wilde away from his decorous married life in Tite Street, Chelsea, and into the arms of paid young men. Neither Oscar nor Bosie was unduly discreet about their adventures, and it may be that the risk of exposure added a thrill to their nights of "feasting with panthers." They were playing with fire, and Queensberry was determined that they would burn.

His opening shot came on the morning of February 28, 1895, just two weeks after Wilde's moment of glory. Queensberry sent a card to "Oscar Wilde, posing Somdomite." (Spelling was not Queensberry's strong point.) War was declared. After briefly considering the option of running to France for refuge, Wilde resolved to fight his case in the courts. Many of his friends warned him that no good could come of it, but his solicitor, Travers Humphreys, and the enraged Bosie egged him on. The next day, Wilde went to the Marlborough Street police station and swore out a warrant for the arrest of Queensberry on a charge of libel.

The courtroom drama that followed fell into three acts. Things might have gone differently for Wilde had Queensberry not been represented by Edward Carson, a brilliant and merciless young barrister, who, like Wilde, had studied at Trinity College, Dublin. Wilde, Over-confident of his wit and skills as a public speaker, regarded Carson flippantly. The crowd loved this display of peacock arrogance, but it was a terrible mistake. Gradually, Carson built such a strong case, with such telling evidence of Wilde's having consorted with rent boys, that the jury was compelled to find Queensberry not guilty. The next step was inevitable. Wilde now stood accused.

The new trial began at the end of April. This time, Wilde was cross-examined by a new lawyer, who began by asking the writer about certain passages in his published works. What, did Wilde mean by the "love that dare not speak its name?" Wilde's reply was eloquent; this "love," he said, "is such a great affection of an elder man for a younger man as there was between David and Jonathan, such as Plato made the very basis of his philosophy, and such as you find in the sonnets of Michelangelo and Shakespeare…" This speech had a powerful effect on the jury, who declared themselves unable to return a verdict. A third and final trial was called.

Wilde was doomed and he probably knew it. He went back into the courtroom on May 22, and the case lasted until the 25th—Queen Victoria's birthday. Broken in spirit, he listened to the vehement denunciations as if they were "like a passage in Dante." Summing up, Justice Alfred Wills declared, "It is the worst case I have ever tried." Wilde was found guilty, and sentenced to the maximum penalty for indecency: two years of hard labor. Voices in the gallery protested—"Shame!"—and Wilde himself, almost choked with despair, managed to ask "And I? May I say nothing, my Lord?" The Judge waved his hand in dismissal, and Wilde was carried away by the wardens, almost unconscious. He was taken straight from the courtroom to prison, where he was stripped, bathed, put in his uniform and locked in a cell. He was ultimately transferred to Pentonville Prison, where his next two years were like a term in Hell, and he spent his time writing a long and angry letter to his former love.

Wilde's later life makes sad reading. Despised and rejected by all but a few brave and loyal friends, he went into voluntary exile in Italy and France, adopting the name "Sebastian Melmoth." There were a few half-hearted efforts to write dramas again, but he was a broken man, ill and humiliatingly poor. He died at 46 on November 30, 1900. Though Bosie served as chief mourner at the funeral, in time even he would denounce his former friend.

CHAPTER 26.

WINSTON CHURCHILL AT THE SIEGE OF SIDNEY STREET

3 JANUARY 1911

Soon, the guns were going to be blazing. Winston Churchill knew that, and he was determined to have some fun.

In the early hours of January 3, 1911, he had received an urgent message from the Metropolitan Police. They were laying siege to a house in the Stepney district of East London. About three weeks earlier, a gang of Latvians had been interrupted by the police while trying to tunnel their way into a jeweler's shop. The Latvians had retaliated with heavy gunfire—a rare criminal act at that time—killing two officers and wounding a third, before escaping and finding a safe house not far away in Sidney Street. Here they had hidden until the police finally tracked them down on the evening of January 2. Meanwhile, London was alive with alarming rumors. The Latvians, they said, were not common thieves but a terrifying band of anarchists. They were certainly recent immigrants, and xenophobia was very much in the air, especially since the restrictive Aliens Bill of 1904.

Even though the police had been issued with firearms, they knew that if they were going to storm the place successfully, they needed reinforcements. Would Churchill, as Home Secretary, recruit an armed platoon of Scots

Winston Churchill, 1904

Guards from the Tower of London? Churchill signed the form without hesitation. He then put on his fine lamb's wool-collared overcoat, donned his top hat, summoned his long-suffering secretary Edward Marsh, and set off into battle by open-topped car—pausing only to be photographed by the press, who knew that Winston always made for good copy.

At the age of 36, Winston Churchill still looked much more like the slim and dashing young officer of Hussars he had been in his early twenties than the growling bulldog he later became. The man who would twice serve as Prime Minister, and would later be elected the "Greatest Briton" of all time, was born into an aristocratic family in their Oxfordshire palace in 1874. Growing up in Dublin, he suffered from a speech impediment and was a poor student; when he applied to the Royal Military College, Sandhurst, he failed the admissions exam three times. When he graduated, he took a post in the cavalry, using family connections to get him into exciting active combat situations and working as a journalist on the side. After service in Cuba, British India and Africa, Churchill returned to England and followed in the footsteps of his father, successfully campaigning for Parliament as a Conservative in 1900.

By the standards of the day, he was a very young man indeed when he was made Home Secretary in 1910—the youngest British politician to take the post since 34-year-old Robert Peel in 1822—and almost everyone who met him commented on his endearing boyishness. He was energetic, driven, possessed of an immense physical courage, and was already noted as a brilliant orator and conversationalist, though cynics observed that his favorite form of talk was the Churchillian monologue. But not everyone was charmed. He also had the gift of being rude, angering people and making lifelong enemies. Most Conservative Members of Parliament disliked him, especially after he left their ranks in 1904 and "crossed the House," as the saying goes, to join the dominant Liberal Party.

The job of Home Secretary — which includes control of the Police and the maintenance of public order — is a tricky one.

Soldiers from the Scots Guards open fire on Sidney Street, 1911

As a later incumbent of the post explained, it means maintaining the delicate balance between the liberty of citizens and the proper power of the state. Ideally, a Home Secretary should be seen as steady, patient and diplomatic, especially at a time when some great issue is dividing the nation. In 1911, that issue was industrial relations: management versus labor. Rightly or wrongly, Churchill was believed to have approached recent industrial negotiations like an ungelded steer in a china shop. A calmer, more mature man would have signed for reinforcements and remained in his office for the rest of the day.

But Home Secretary Churchill was, under his astrakhan coat, very much the same publicity-hungry war correspondent and soldier who would cheerfully travel on a hot, cramped train for five weeks just to join a bloody campaign for a few days, who had hugely enjoyed coming under fire in Cuba on his twenty-first birthday, who had shown his bravery again and again by hurling himself into combat in India, Egypt and South Africa. He was well aware of that fact that his presence at the Stepney siege would be a magnet for the press, and that awareness added to his exhilaration.

It isn't clear whether Churchill took direct control of the siege operations, though he probably did not issue any orders to the police. The troops and the constables opened fire, and the Latvians returned with equal force. (One story has it that a bullet whizzed straight through Churchill's top hat.) Another officer was killed, and two more were wounded. Before long, the safe house caught fire. The head of the fire brigade asked for Churchill's

Detectives from Scotland Yard inspect the burning house at the center of the Siege of Sidney Street

orders: Should he send his men in and risk the possibility of them being shot? Churchill told him to let the house burn to the ground. When the blaze finally died out, the police discovered two charred bodies among the ashes, which meant that at least one Latvian must have escaped.

Had they so chosen, the press might have made Churchill out to be the hero of the day—a man not frightened to put his skin at risk in the public interest. Instead, they decided to make him the fool or the villain of the piece. At best, he was an irresponsible statesman who had not yet learned to leave the task of law enforcement to the police, at worst an overgrown boy scout. His parliamentary colleagues were in little doubt about Churchill's lust for the limelight. Two weeks later, when Churchill reported on these events in the House of Commons, one of his colleagues made a coolly insolent remark about a photo of Churchill peering round the corner of a house at the shootout. "I understand what the photographer was doing, but what was the Right Honourable Gentleman doing?"

It was a political blunder on Churchill's part, but a blunder with unexpectedly happy consequences. The Liberals decided that he was temperamentally unsuited to the peaceful arts of Home Secretary, so they shifted him to the far more suitable post of First Lord of the Admiralty. And, as most of his biographers have agreed, the personal courage and matchless self-confidence which had shown so poorly in 1911 were the very qualities that would make him exactly the right man to be Prime Minister of his country three decades later.

LONDON IN PAINTING

1.

2.

3.

4.

5.

6.

1. *Westminster Bridge from the North on Lord Mayor's Day*, by Canaletto, 1746, Yale Center for British Art, New Haven **2.** *The Thames and the City of London from Richmond House*, by Canaletto, 1746, Private Collection **3.** *The Mall in St. James's Park*, by Thomas Gainsborough, c. 1783 The Frick Collection, New York **4.** *Old London Bridge*, by Joseph Mallord William Turner, 1796-97, Tate Britain **5.** *View Of The City Of London From Sir Richard Steele's Cottage, Hampstead*, by John Constable, c. 1832, Yale Center for British Art, New Haven **6.** *The Thames at Westminster*, by Claude Monet, 1871, National Gallery London

CHAPTER 27

THE BLITZ

7 SEPTEMBER 1940 AND 10 MAY 1941

Imagine the terror. It was five in the afternoon on September 7, 1940, and the day was still bright when Londoners heard a rumbling from the east, looked up into the skies, and saw the most terrible sight the ancient town had ever witnessed. The sky suddenly grew dark, not with storm clouds but with aircraft; no fewer than 600 German planes, bombers and fighters, flying in wave upon wave of attack formations that stretched some 12 miles wide. The bomb bay doors opened and the instruments of death rained down: high explosives to shatter buildings and tear apart bodies, and incendiary devices that created firestorms too ferocious for emergency services to fight.

The Nazi forces wanted to destroy the London docks, the city's essential lifeline in both peace and war, so they hit the working-class areas of the East End's docklands district. It all went up in flames. One observer said that that the Thames, reflecting vast walls of fire along its banks, looked like a lake in the middle of Hell. It was appalling, horrific, obscene. And the very next day, it began all over again. For 57 consecutive nights.

American war correspondents wrote home about the cruel magnificence of the spectacle of a whole city blazing in the night. At closer quarters, the

⟨ Children made homeless by the Blitz sit admid the rubble of an eastern suburb of London, September 1940.

St. Paul's during the Blitz by Herbert Mason

horror and the heartbreak were all but unspeakable. Rescue teams, mostly civilian, crawled through burning wreckage to bring out babies and toddlers who would never know their parents. Let one unnamed female volunteer's testimony stand for many thousands. This young woman had been an art student before the war, and her knowledge of anatomy was now being put to macabre use.

"We had somehow to form a body for burial so that the relatives (without seeing it) could imagine that their loved one was more or less intact for that purpose. But it was a very difficult task—there were so many pieces missing and, as one of the mortuary attendants said, 'proper jigsaw puzzle, ain't it, Miss?' The stench was the worst thing about it…I think this task dispelled for me the idea that human life is valuable."

By the time Blitzkrieg ("Lightning War") ended—about eight months later, on the night of May 10 to 11, 1941—28,566 Londoners had been killed and another 25,578 wounded. No other British city lost as many souls.

Winston Churchill had predicted in 1934 that the city "must expect that, under the pressure of constant attack upon London, at least three or four

Left: Air Chief Marshal Sir Hugh Dowding accompanying King George VI and the future Queen Elizabeth II during a visit to Bently Priory, 1940; Right: A scene from the propaganda film *London Can Take It*

million people would be driven out into the open country around the metropolis." Other military strategists came to the even more pessimistic conclusion that sustained bombing would destroy all public order; there would be a complete breakdown of stability, and the country would be powerless to resist invasion. The Germans thought along the same lines. Their concerted bombing of Britain, known to the Nazi High Command as Operation Luge, after the Wagnerian fire god, was to have been the prelude to Operation Sea Lion—a full-scale campaign of invasion.

The so-called "Myth of the Blitz" began to take form while the bombing was still going on, thanks in part to the documentary filmmakers like the brilliant young director Humphrey Jennings, who took their cameras out on the blazing streets and recorded the gentle courage and lightheartedness of Londoners. Films like *London Can Take It* were shipped around the world, particularly to the still-neutral United States, to show that Dr. Joseph Goebbels's claims of imminent British defeat were hollow.

To the exasperation of the German high command, the daily atrocities did not reduce London to panic or revolt. Under the command of Hugh Dowding, the Royal Air Force—or to be exact, the No. 11 Fighter Group, the division assigned to protect the capital—fought back with a heroism that is still warmly remembered and annually commemorated on September 15, Battle of Britain Day. (Fighter Command had been dueling with the Luftwaffe throughout the hot summer leading up to the Blitz; "Spitfire

Summer," it was called.) On that day in 1940, the young pilots, more than half of them volunteers, retaliated against two major daytime attacks on London, shooting down almost a fifth of the Luftwaffe's planes. Two days later, Adolf Hitler officially postponed Operation Sea Lion, and he never took up those plans again.

The Battle of Britain was a much-needed boost to morale, but there was no shortage of horror ahead, as the attacks now began to come by night rather than day. One of the most dreadful nights was December

West End Air Raid Shelter

29, when 130 German bombers unloaded more than 100,000 incendiary bombs over the oldest part of London, the City. The conflagration soon became known as the Second Great Fire; one of the few buildings to escape destruction was St. Paul's. A photograph of its dome illuminated by flames taken by Herbert Mason became a pictorial emblem of survival against the odds. The destruction stretched from Islington to St. Paul's churchyard—much larger than the fire zone in 1666. The miraculous survival of St. Paul's was treated as a kind of assurance from God that Britain would prevail; but the miracle had a good deal of help from Churchill, who had issued the order that St. Paul's was to be saved "at all costs."

Churchill proved invaluable to this heroic resistance. The lifetime politician had long been a hated figure among the British left because of his hardline anti-union policies and his hostility to the General Strike, but when Prime Minister Neville Chamberlain resigned on May 10, 1940, Churchill was seen as someone who could unite leaders on all sides of British politics. He had warned for years about the threat posed by Hitler, and as war loomed, King George VI asked Churchill to assume the post of Prime Minister.

One MP on the far left recalled that in secret Parliamentary sessions, Churchill "was at his greatest ... He would share with us facts and figures which seemed, on any basis of logic, to add up to inevitable and imminent disaster. But his own stubborn courage made nonsense of logic, and we would troop out of the House at the end of the debate feeling that Britain was invincible." Churchill's sublime rhetorical skills and incomparable charisma made the whole nation feel that his vision was also theirs.

In recent years, some historians have tried to show that the image of a bold, unwavering and cheerful London was in some measure fiction, deliberately cultivated by the government and its propaganda agencies to keep the population from feeling doomed and ripe for surrender. There is a degree of truth in such revisionist views. Some Londoners panicked, others took to crime. In the early days of the Blitz there were suicides; bombed houses were looted and the black market thrived; prostitutes did a roaring trade in the blacked-out streets.

Even wartime equality had its limits. Some rich people fled the capital for the relative safety of their houses in the countryside. (Indeed, some of the affection for the Royal Family in the years since the Blitz is due to the fact that the King and Queen did not run from danger, but stayed in London while the bombs fell. The Queen said that she felt a certain pride when Buckingham Palace was hit: now, she said, she and the King could "look the East End in the face.") Snobbish, middle-class officials sometimes refused to allow poor people to seek shelter in the Underground stations, until they were forced to give in by agitation from the Communist Party. And so on. The experience of war did not altogether lead to a ceasefire in the ancient war between classes.

And yet there are plenty of testimonies by diary keepers and letter writers that many Londoners really did feel that they were suddenly united—like brothers and sisters who had for the time being dropped their usual petty family quarrels and joined ranks. Noël Coward wrote a sentimental song about this experience of unity, and called it "London Pride." Typical of Coward's sensibility, the sinister word "Blitz" is rhymed with "Ritz": "Every Blitz its resistance stiffening/From the Ritz to the Anchor and Crown"—the latter name evoking some jovial cockney pub. It's a little silly, but few Londoners can hear it without a twinge of raw emotion. Those eight bloody, terrifying, tragic months when Britain was the one nation standing up against the nightmarish forces of the Third Reich is a good enough reason for Londoners to feel justly proud of their home.

CHAPTER 28

THE BEATLES FINISH RECORDING "SGT. PEPPER'S LONELY HEARTS CLUB BAND"

1 APRIL 1967

"Nobody likes a smart-arse," John Lennon sneered at the Beatles' jack-of-all trades, Neil Aspinall. But for once, the chronically sarcastic Beatle, the Hard One, was only kidding. "That," Aspinall remembers, "was when I knew that John liked [the song] and that it would happen." They were all in Abbey Road Studios, and the Beatles had just finished recording the last track of the album *Sgt. Pepper's Lonely Hearts Club Band*—a quick reprise of the title song, to be tucked on to side two of the album, just before "A Day in the Life." Aspinall had suggested to Paul McCartney that the reprise might help pull the album together, so they gave it a shot. The recording had taken less than a day—the band was under pressure from their record company, EMI, to finish the album after months of recording sessions—and some people claim that you can still hear the excitement of the studio in the finished song.

As they walked out of Abbey Road with an acetate proof of the new album, dawn was breaking over St. John's Wood. Going home would be too much of an anti-climax, so they piled into cars and drove a few miles across town to Chelsea, where their American friend "Mama" Cass Elliot, of the Mamas and the Papas, was staying in a flat just off the King's Road. This was the summer of "Swinging London" and the King's Road was the place to be.

Cass Elliot

It was April 1, 1967, April Fool's Day, and the sun was already up by six a.m. Wanting to share their masterpiece with the world, John Lennon, Paul McCartney, George Harrison and Ringo Starr opened the windows wide, wrangled some giant speakers out onto the roof and cranked up the volume. Normally, the "straights" in the neighborhood would have been outraged, but instead there was an almost miraculous wave of good will. "All the windows around us opened," a friend of the band recalled, "and people leaned out, wondering. It was obvious who it was on the record. Nobody complained. A lovely spring morning. People were smiling and giving us the thumbs up."

It was an unexpectedly happy ending, and one that almost no one could have predicted before, when the Beatles had come perilously close to breaking up. They had been forced into a grueling, humiliating regime of tours that left them exhausted and angry; President Ferdinand Marcos's goon squads had roughed them up during a tour of the Philippines; outraged Christians across the United States were making bonfires of their records and merchandise after word got out that Lennon had made some throwaway remark about the Beatles being more popular than Jesus. When asked by a British journalist about their future plans, Harrison had glumly responded, "We'll take a couple of weeks to recuperate before we go and get beaten up by the Americans." He was exaggerating, but only a little—the Beatles' third and final American tour had been a depressing trail of half-empty venues and botched management. Lennon came close to cracking and would shriek incomprehensible obscenities into the microphone. At the end of the tour, Harrison told their manager, Brian Epstein, that he was quitting.

Sgt. Pepper was that it was a chance for the four young men to draw breath, and learn to enjoy making music again. They also learned to enjoy each other's company, and the *Pepper* sessions were almost astonishingly harmonious. People who saw them at the time noted that they were now operating as though they were telepathically linked, thinking the same thoughts without needing to put them into words. Part of this communion was due to Lennon's experiences with LSD, which had helped calm his rage and violence but left him dreamy and reliant on the other Beatles to keep him on the ground. "If I'm on my own for three days, doing nothing, I almost leave myself completely. I'm up there watching myself or I'm at the back of my head. I can see my hands and realize they're moving, but it's a robot who's doing it." McCartney admitted to sharing similar feelings.

The music that they were producing was a very long way from the driving, infectious beat that had made them famous. Musically, it drew on everything from old-time Music Hall songs to Tin Pan Alley ballads, from rock and roll to Indian classical music and the European avant-garde. People who recall the oddities of Lennon's collaboration with Yoko Ono tend to think of him as the experimental Beatle, but at this stage it was McCartney who was taking a keen interest in the likes of Stockhausen and Luciano Berio. Lyrically, it was the work of magpies, full of overheard or remembered phrases, and based on quite trivial events from their daily lives—like McCartney's meeting with Meta Davis (a traffic warden in a nearby street in St. John's Wood), an encounter which gave rise to the song "Lovely Rita." Lennon later said that he despised these "novelistic" songs by his former friend: "These stories about boring people doing boring things—being postmen and secretaries and writing home. I'm not interested in third-party songs. I like to write about me, coz I *know* me…"

The most "me" of Lennon's songs on *Pepper* is "A Day in the Life," which is cobbled together from all sorts of disparate elements in his life at the time. It begins with an allusion to the Beatles' young millionaire friend Tara Browne, who, on December 18, 1966, high on drugs, drove his sports car through a red light in South Kensington, crashed into a van and killed himself. A reference to the "English army" winning the war alludes to Lennon's acting role in the film *How I Won the War*. And so on. It is a doom-filled song, and many of the other songs on the album are melancholy and wistful. Yet the overall mood of *Pepper* is one of euphoria and affirmation; in the years since its release the record has been voted, over and over, the greatest album of all time. No wonder the inhabitants of Chelsea smiled as its melodies greeted the spring morning.

LET IT BE

Even the most die-hard fan couldn't buy a ticket to The Beatles's last public performance. In fact, it was totally unannounced, a mid-afternoon gig atop the roof of the Apple Records building at 3 Savile Row in Mayfair.

By the end of the '60s things were tense between the Beatles. John Lennon and Paul McCartney had been the Beatles' breakout stars and they wielded that power over the band, often disagreeing with one another. The sessions for *The Beatles* (The White Album) had been the most difficult yet, but after just a few months the band was back in the studio.

In January 1969, the Fab Four started work on *Let it Be* and, along with the album, they filmed rehearsal and recording sessions for a fly-on-the wall style documentary about the workings of the band. But they couldn't agree on anything. Lennon wanted his songs on a separate side of the album from McCartney's; George Harrison walked out for a week.

They had planned to culminate with a one-off concert, but no one could agree on where—suggestions included a London club, onboard a ship and in the North African desert. Finally, the fed-up band decided to stay close to home and set up a show on the roof of their studio. On the overcast afternoon of January 30, 1969, they played five songs from five stories high, including "Get Back" and "Don't Let Me Down," before police came and stopped them.

Let it Be was released on May 8, 1970, just eight months after the release of *Abbey Road*, which was actually recorded after it. By then, the band had announcement that they were splitting. *Let it Be* includes one song recorded on that final rooftop concert, "One After 909." The album won a Grammy for Best Original Soundtrack.

CHAPTER 29.

JOHNNY ROTTEN AUDITIONS FOR THE SEX PISTOLS
AUGUST 1975

John Lydon was a scrawny kid, with decayed teeth, cropped hair and a strange, unnerving gaze that was the legacy of the meningitis he had contracted at the age of eight. Adding to his odd appearance were his clothes, which had been deliberately ripped up and festooned with safety pins—an urchin, a neo-Dickensian look that within a matter of months would be visible on every street in London. His Catholic parents were immigrants from Ireland (Galway, Cork), and until quite recently he had been living with them in the depressing North London district of Finsbury Park, drifting aimlessly in and out of education and menial jobs. Almost no one would have seen star potential in this thin, sarcastic youth, but an older man called Malcolm McLaren was intrigued by the swagger Lydon displayed when he wandered into McLaren's clothes shop SEX, at 430 King's Road, Chelsea.

McLaren—an art school graduate who had picked up on a few of the revolutionary ideas that were coming out of Paris from the late 1960s onwards—had already enjoyed a lively and profitable career as a designer of "alternative" clothes, in collaboration with his partner Vivienne Westwood. SEX was just the latest incarnation of a store that changed styles as

Punks near Camden Market, London

frequently as McLaren took up fads and then dropped them. It began as Let It Rock, an outlet for a retro-1950s look based on the London Teddy Boy fashion of twenty years earlier—long draped coats, string ties, big "brothel-creeper" shoes. In 1973, the place mutated into Too Fast to Live Too Young to Die and began to specialise in an earlier look still—the American Zoot Suits of the 1940s. The following year, No. 430 was reborn as SEX. This time the emphasis was on provocation—more of the social than the erotic kind—and SEX specialised in variants of traditional fetish wear: rubber and vinyl, bondage trousers, chains, t-shirts printed with images from both gay and straight porn—most famously, an image by Tom of Finland of two men in cowboy gear, naked from the waist down, their penises almost touching. It was calculated to make the middle-aged and respectable foam with rage. Kids loved it.

Britain in 1975 was more than ripe for another youth rebellion. By July, the country was in a deep recession and unemployment figures were the worst they had been since the end of the War, with over 1 million people out of work nationwide. By the end of the year, Chancellor Denis Healey had to present Parliament with proposed budget cuts of three billion pounds. It was hard for the young and under-educated to find jobs; which meant that there was a lot of free time and surplus energy available for tapping. The SEX business was booming, but McLaren was highly ambitious. A brief trip to Manhattan and an entanglement with the New York Dolls gave him an idea: an entirely new kind of rock group, calculated to enrage the public rather than woo it. He had already had a trio of likely lads on hand: Steve Jones and Paul Cook, oafish fellows from Shepherd's Bush (a working-class area of West London that had spawned The Who in the early 1960s), and the quieter, more educated Glen Matlock. What McLaren needed was a front man. He invited Lydon to meet the others at a nearby pub, the Roebuck.

It did not start well. Jones and the others didn't like the supercilious, sneering tone that Lydon took towards them; Lydon himself later admitted that he was terrified. But McLaren put a microphone into his hand and ordered him to sing along to a record on the juke box: "Eighteen," by Alice Cooper. Initially hesitant, Lydon suddenly exploded into a series of wild actions that earlier ages might have read as the signs of demonic possession. He screamed, crouched like a hunchback, rolled on the floor, bucked and went into spasms and pretended to puke. It was electrifying and, to the onlookers, savagely funny. Jones and Cook still hated him, but McLaren knew that he had found his frontman. No matter that Lydon couldn't really sing and had no sense of rhythm. He had something more important: charisma.

The Sex Pistols were ready to be loaded, aimed and fired at the unsuspecting public. One of them, Matlock, was soon fired in another sense, for being too fond of melody and musicianship. He was replaced by the obnoxious John Ritchie, soon renamed Sid Vicious. The next couple of years were tumultuous, and ended in conspicuous failure (the Pistols' first and only American tour was a flop). And yet this scruffy quartet, and their manager McLaren, made an impact vastly in excess of their record sales, while Lydon—renamed "Johnny Rotten" because of his disgusting teeth—became one of the most hated men in Britain. Though their earliest gigs drew only small numbers of people, lots of those people went off and formed bands of their own: the Clash, the Buzzcocks, the Slits, Siouxie and the Banshees. Punk, a word which meant "prostitute" in Shakespeare's day and a cheap criminal in more recent times, now designated a defiantly crude and messy musical style, a dress code—all over Britain, boys and girls had their long hair slashed back and styled into aggressive spikes—and an attitude compounded of sullenness, defiance and ill-thought-out nihilism. Traditional adolescent traits, presented with a new kind of theatricality.

One of the positive side of punk was that it said there was nothing special about being a rock star, and that there was no intrinsic merit in virtuosity, especially not the brand of virtuosity which had dominated the musical scene of the early 1970s: Yes, Genesis, ELP, Pink Floyd. (The first time McLaren spotted Lydon, he was wearing a Pink Floyd t-shirt on which he had scrawled the words "I Hate.") One fanzine of the time ran a front cover which showed crude diagrams of guitar fingerings. "Here's a chord," the caption read. "Here's another. Here's a third. Now form a band." And many readers did just that. Punk could also be funny and exciting, and like other kinds of popular music throughout the twentieth century, it gave teenagers a way of making their parents very angry indeed.

The darker side was an undercurrent of violence, which began in some of the earliest Sex Pistols gigs at venues such as the 100 Club on Oxford Street and El Paradise, a Soho strip club. In one nasty incident, a well-known rock journalist, Nick Kent, was threatened with a knife by one of Rotten's friends, and then had his face slashed with a bicycle chain wielded by Sid Vicious. Not that all the violence came from the punks. In the summer of 1977, when the Pistol's cacophonous, jeering song "God Save the Queen" topped the singles charts during the week of Her Majesty's Silver Jubilee celebrations, Rotten was attacked by a patriotic street gang. Violent rhetoric inspired violent reality, and the uglier side of punk culminated in the downfall of Sid Vicious—a descent into heroin addiction that led to the bloody death of his American girlfriend, Nancy Spungen, in New York's infamous Hotel Chelsea. Vicious was accused of murder and arrested. He made bail a few months later, but died of a heroin overdose his first night out. His mother found a suicide note in the pocket of his jacket. By then, Rotten had quit the band, leaving McLaren and the others to keep squeezing money out of the public with increasingly self-parodying gestures.

Lydon had a quick intelligence, but he was poorly schooled; McLaren was the closest thing to an intellectual in the gang, and he went on to execute a number of strange projects, none of them as successful as the Pistols, but some quite interesting. He directed a film about the history of Oxford Street, scene of some of the band's most notorious performances, and suggested that the place bore the ghostly traces of previous inhabitants, from highwaymen to the Romantic opium addict, Thomas de Quincey. McLaren sometimes said that the Pistols had been a phenomenon that only London could have produced, and that they were like a late-twentieth century manifestation of

Jamie Reid's *God Save The Queen* poster

that ancient spirit of revolt by the London underclass that has erupted again and again across the centuries. He may have been right.

SUBCULTURES OF LONDON

Through the second half of the twentieth century, London has exported a series of subcultures in music and fashion with unusually wide-ranging influence.

Beginning in the '50s and peaking in the mid-'60s, mods (short for modernists) rebelled against old-fashioned English ideals. Mods found style inspiration in Italian magazines, favoring custom-made Italian suits for the guys and mini-skirts and figure-hugging sweaters for the girls. They listened to the emerging R&B sounds from coffeehouse jukeboxes, made scooters *en vogue* and were the first to be associated with amphetamine-fueled all-night dancing (referenced in the stuttering delivery of The Who's "My Generation"). A second wave revived Mod style back in the 1970s with acts like The Jam and the film *Quadrophenia*.

As mods adopted more elaborate fashions, skins, or skinheads, emerged out of the working class, adopting a uniform of slim jeans and Dr. Martens boots and shaving their heads in response to the wider hippie and psychedelic culture. Early skins were were heavily influenced by Jamaican rude boy culture and ska music, but nationalist politics would later come to define the movement.

With their safety-pinned clothes, spiked hair and anarchist attitudes, the punks of the mid-1970s were born of the decade's bleak economic outlook and were heralded by the Sex Pistols. By the late '70s and early '80s, a reactionary evolution to the punk movement had developed, the New Romantics, characterized by their glam rock roots and heavy use of synthesizers to make lush synthpop compositions.

CHAPTER 30

PRINCE WILLIAM MARRIES CATHERINE MIDDLETON

29 APRIL 2011

Some say that only three hundred million watched the proceedings; some estimate that it was as many as two billion. Precise figures hardly count. The significant fact is that, in 2011, very large numbers of people from many nations retained enough interest in the British monarchy to drop their regular viewing habits—and, for some, their sleeping habits—to watch a wedding between offspring from the grand family of Mountbatten-Windsor (William) and one from the somewhat less illustrious family of Middleton (Catherine). This keen attention would have surprised many of William's famous ancestors, and might well have amazed Queen Victoria, who realized in the course of her long widowhood that she was growing ever more unpopular, and the likelihood of a British Republic was ever more real.

As George Orwell noted during World War II, in his brilliant essay about British culture, "The Lion and the Unicorn," the country—like its capital city—has the paradoxical capacity both to change beyond all recognition and yet stay in essence much the same. Kate and William's wedding is a fitting example. If the ghost of the monarch who rebuilt Westminster Abbey, Henry III, was present at the nuptials, he would surely have been baffled by the lights, cameras, television crews and general trappings of advanced technology. But at the heart of the spectacle was something wholly familiar, and central to London's history: the marriage of a Crown Prince.

If Henry's ghost then left the Abbey and wandered along the banks of the Thames, he would have seen a great deal to astonish him, much of it the product of the late twentieth and early twenty-first centuries. Across the river, he would have seen one of London's newest landmarks: the London Eye, a giant Ferris wheel lit up for the occasion in the red, white and blue of the Union Flag. Londoners have taken this structure to their hearts in a way that is unusual for new buildings, and so have tourists—three and a half million visitors pay to ride on it every year. (The thirty-two capsules in which passengers ride represent the thirty-two boroughs of London.) It was built as one of the Millennium celebrations, and was meant only to be a temporary attraction, but it is now so firmly identified with the London skyline that films and television shows—like the BBC's updated version of the Sherlock Holmes adventures—now use it in their title sequences as an instant recognizable signifier of the town.

The Eye is just one of the many new additions to the London skyline, evidence of a city transforming yet again as it enters another new century. One of the city's new icons is the Gherkin, designed by the architecture firm of Sir Norman Foster and completed in 2003. More formally known as the Swiss Re Building, or 30 St. Mary Axe, the curvy, glittering creation resembles a plump space rocket from a 1950s science fiction film, and owes its affectionate nickname to its supposed resemblance to a green pickle. A less affectionate nickname was given to another building designed by Foster + Partners, the new London City Hall in Southwark, near Tower Bridge, which opened in 2002. The left-wing former Mayor of London, Ken Livingstone, notoriously called this globular structure "the glass testicle." His Tory successor, the conspicuously eccentric and wild-haired Boris Johnson, softened this a little to "the glass gonad," and the still more polite "onion."

Such hi-tech structures are the proof of the blossoming British architecture has undergone in the past three decades or so—the towering figures in the revival are Norman Foster, Sir Richard Rogers and the late James Stirling. Today, British architects are in demand all over the world, from Germany to Hong Kong. There are various reasons for this renaissance. One of them

The London Eye

is a predictable aesthetic reaction against the "New Brutalist" architecture of the 1960s and 1970s, with its monolithic concrete blocks, puritanical horror of decorative detail and general air of Stalinist gloom. Another is the advance of building technologies, which allows architects to create grand but elegant essays in shiny glass and shiny metal. And yet another is the boom in London's financial sector: Many of the new buildings house banks and brokerage firms. These great new cathedrals are temples of wealth, not religion.

Another new landmark, the Renzo Piano-designed "Shard of Glass" (a.k.a. 32, London Bridge), is the tallest building not only in London, but in the

London past and present: London Bridge and City Hall

European Union: 72 stories, 1,017 feet high. This puts it well ahead of the previous London champion, the pyramid-topped skyscraper formally known as One, Canada Square, which dominates the Canary Wharf developments in Docklands. Yet another now-famous London structure is the formerly-titled Millennium Dome—designed by Richard Rogers, officially opened for the start of 2000 but in fact dogged by all manner of setbacks and misfortunes. The early career of the Dome was almost farcically unsuccessful—a farce well detailed in the writer Iain Sinclair's furious polemic "Sorry Meniscus." A bare fraction of the predicted crowds turned up to see the " Experience" show, and for several years, the Dome was an all-too-visible embarrassment for Tony Blair's New Labour regime, who had commissioned it. But in 2005, the Dome was rented by the O2 group and has rapidly become a highly successful venue for large-scale concerts, sporting and entertainment events, which generated nearly 16 million pounds in pre-tax profit in its first full year of operation.

London has loved spectacles and excelled at mounting them, from Henry V's triumphal return after Agincourt to the wedding in 1981 of Prince Charles to Lady Diana Spencer—and the still more extraordinary sight of her funeral in 1997, an event that was stage-managed by the traditional institutions of Church and State, but was acted out mainly by the people of London, in a massive, spontaneous eruption of mourning. There had been nothing remotely like it since the funeral of Winston Churchill, three decades earlier. And in 2012, the eyes of the world once again were cast on London to see what the old city of royal spectacles could make of the democratic, modern spectacle of an Olympic Games—this time under the artistic direction of one of England's most talented filmmakers, Danny Boyle, the Oscar-winning director of such films as *Trainspotting* and *Slumdog Millionaire*.

Most of London's long life has been conducted in a middle zone between the charming, almost fairy-tale romance of royal love-matches and the frightening but usually small-scale outburst of crime and violence. London in the twenty-first century is one of the safest major cities in the world— much safer by far than it was in the eighteenth century, or during Dickens's childhood. It is much cleaner than in the nineteenth century (the dense fogs of Sherlock Holmes and Jack the Ripper ended with the Clean Air Acts of the 1950s), and, despite a global economic crisis, much more affluent than it was after the Second World War.

Always a multi-cultural city, London has also thrived over the last half-century from the skills, entrepreneurial initiative and rich cultural heritage of new Londoners with backgrounds in Asia, Africa and elsewhere. Today, salmon swim in the increasingly clean Thames water once again as they did when the Romans lived and fished here. And as those hundreds of millions of people watched the likely future king of England marry at Westminster, they witnessed the British monarchy stepping into the future in the center of an ever evolving metropolis. In other words, though Londoners always love to complain about the noise, the overcrowding, the horrific expense and the inconvenience of their hometown, a dispassionate judge would have to say that, if (as the famous Cockney phrase went) "fings ain't wot they used ter be," then they have changed for the better as well as the worse. London is still one of the world's great cities.

LONDON
WALKING TOURS

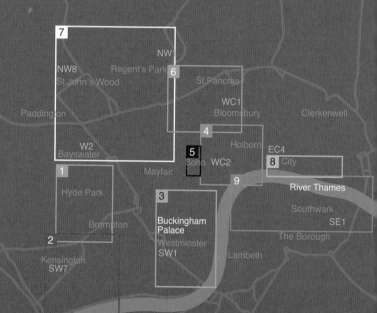

Greater London

KENSINGTON AND KNIGHTSBRIDGE

START:
Kensington Gardens

TUBE:
🚇 Lancaster Gate

END:
One Hyde Park

TUBE:
🚇 Knightsbridge

Kensington Palace

A walk through Kensington and Knightsbridge surveys some of the most expensive and posh parts of London, passing through the city's most intense concentration of museums and ritzy shopping areas. It is a district that has long been home to some of Britain's wealthiest citizens—and a few embassies—and is a marketplace for its residents' every upscale desire. Much of the area is grand and Victorian, some of it is surprisingly intimate, and there are plenty of quiet spaces along the way for restful stops.

1 Begin at Lancaster Gate underground station and stroll across Kensington Gardens, starting from its charming Italian Garden to the north. The water garden, with its four fountains, ponds and many statues, marks the beginning of the Serpentine, a body of water that stretches south and then west into Hyde Park.

2 About halfway along the west bank is a modest statue of Peter Pan, which marks the spot where the fictional sprite Peter touches down on Earth in J. M. Barrie's first story, published in 1902. The Peter Pan stories were inspired by Barrie's friendship with the Llewelyn Davies family—in particular, their small son Michael—who lived nearby. It is said that the idea of Peter Pan came to Barrie when he saw Michael playing near the Round Pond.

3 The next landmark along the banks is the Serpentine Gallery, which opened in 1970. This is something of an avant-garde wolf in teashop clothing, and it is a beloved stalwart of cutting-edge culture. Behind its genteel exterior, it is a display place for exhibitions by modern artists both dead (Andy Warhol, Man Ray, Louise Bourgeois) and living (Anish Kapoor, Damien Hirst, Gerhard Richter). Every summer, the gallery invites world-class architects to create a temporary pavilion of striking design, and there is also a permanent display of outdoor works by the major Scottish artist Ian Hamilton Finlay, dedicated to the memory of Princess Diana.

Princess Diana

4 Just opposite the gallery and across the road is the Gardens' newest landmark, the Diana, Princess of Wales Memorial Fountain. Designed with the Princess's "openness" in mind, the memorial has allowed, banned, then re-allowed visitors to wade in its waters since its opening in 2004.

5 Another artwork worth looking for is the Albert Memorial, a highly decorated lump of ornamentation devoted to Queen Victoria's beloved prince consort. The monument features carvings and figures representing England's Victorian-era achievements and Albert's love of the arts.

Queen Victoria and Prince Albert, 1854

Dated 1911, this City of Westminster milestone sits on the south side of Knightsbridge to the east of Royal Albert Hall.

6 Opposite the memorial is the unmissable Royal Albert Hall (opened in 1871), one of London's major musical venues, which used to be described as having everything a concert hall needed…except decent acoustics. The attempts to remedy the echo and troublesome acoustics were numerous, with the most recent improvements occurring between 1998 and 2003. If you are visiting in the summer months, make an effort to attend one of the BBC's Promenade Concerts, or "Proms," which vary in quality from the merely good to the utterly sublime. The famous "Last Night of the Proms" is a time for pomp and high-spirited singing of patriotic songs, climaxing with "Land of Hope and Glory." Fun!

Albert's name is all over this district, and deservedly so, since it was Victoria's beloved prince consort who determined that profits from the 1851 Great Exhibition should be devoted to centers of wholesome instruction and empowerment. His ambitions originally extended to a full-scale development of a large block of land between Hyde Park and South Kensington; the large museums which survive there were part of this "Albertopolis" scheme.

7 To the east you will be able to see the tower of Hyde Park Barracks, home to the men (and their families) and horses of the Household Cavalry. The site has seen several versions of the barracks since the 1790s; the tower was completed in 1970. Designed by Sir Basil Spence, it is an unexpectedly pleasing example of late 1960s and early 1970s architecture, with an interesting balance between plain monumental slabs and decorative detail. Some of its original design has been spoiled by security additions, a response to terrorist attacks by the Irish Republican Army.

8 Walk down Exhibition Road, at the end of which lies South Kensington and three major — and free — museums: the Science Museum, the Natural History Museum and the Victoria and Albert Museum, three of the best museums in the world. Children enjoy the first two. Founded in 1857, the Science Museum boasts free features and an IMAX theater, and its exhibitions range on topics from astronomy to biology.

9 Just past the Science Museum, the Natural History Museum (created by Alfred Waterhouse between 1873 and 1881) celebrates the natural world and spreads the message of environmentalism. Among the museum's most celebrated exhibitions is Dippy, the museum's famous life-sized plaster replica of a fossilized Diplodocus dinosaur skeleton, which greets visitors in the museum's Central Hall. The I Love Dippy appeal, a recent fundraising effort to renovate Central Hall, relies on visitors and friends of the museum to make donations in the hopes of reaching the fundraising goal of £8.5 million.

Dippy was unveiled at the British Museum of Natural History, May 12, 1905.

10 Directly across the road stands the Victoria and Albert Museum, which bills itself as the world's greatest museum of art and design. Built the year after the Great Exhibition, its original title was the Museum of Manufactures. Thanks to generous funding and little competition, its collections grew quite rapidly. The museum became dedicated to the complete history of art and design, acquiring and amassing over the years a vast amount of remarkable works of fine and decorative arts, as well as photography, clothing, textiles, jewelry, ironwork and assorted other global artifacts from both ancient and modern times. The museum was renamed in 1899 when Queen Victoria, in her last official public

Wealthy Londoners shop at Harrods, 1909

Diana and Dodi Memorial at Harrods

outing, laid the foundation stone to the museum's new façade and main entrance.

11 Head northeast along Brompton Road on your way to the temples of luxury that dominate Knightsbridge, including Harrods and the competing Harvey Nichols. Located at Hans Road, Harrods is the United Kingdom's biggest department store—nearly twice as large as its closest rival. If you plan simply to check out Harrods, rather than bankrupt yourself there, don't miss the Food Hall and its Arts and Crafts tiling. Make sure to be smartly dressed, though; the department store is not shy about kicking out or refusing entry to would-be patrons who don't meet its strict dress code.

Between 1984 and 1985, Egyptian billionaire Mohamed Al-Fayed bought complete ownership House of Fraser, the company that owned, among other stores, Harrods. In the summer of 1997, Fayed's son, Dodi, began dating Princess Diana; the two died together in a car crash in Paris that August. To honor their memories (and reinforce his ties to the beloved princess), Fayed commissioned two memorials for Harrods including a candle-lit shrine to the couple—featuring a lipstick-smudged wine glass and a ring bought by Dodi—on the lower ground floor. Originally intended for only two weeks, the memorial remains a fixture by the store's famous Egyptian escalator. In 2005, a statue called *Innocent Victims* was installed at door 3. In 2010, Fayed sold the store to Qatar Holdings for a reported £1.5 billion.

12 At the end of Brompton Road, continue to the corner of Sloane Street and Knightsbridge to shop at Harvey Nichols, a.k.a. "Harvey Nicks." A purveyor

of luxury goods since 1813, when Nichols began selling fine linens, the shop now caters to a younger, more fashion-forward crowd. If fashion isn't your thing, the store's top floor is home to a restaurant, café and wine shop.

13 Across the intersection stands the latest landmark in Knightsbridge: One Hyde Park, a huge complex of retail outlets and apartments for the astronomically wealthy, with views of Harrods and Harvey Nichols to the south, the Serpentine to the north and Buckingham Palace to the east. Such prime real estate is not without its heavy cost. In 2010, a penthouse apartment at One Hyde Park was said to have sold for £140 million, though there may have been a touch of hyperbole in the report.

Here you will find the Knightsbridge underground station on the Piccadilly line.

CHELSEA

1 Cadogan Hotel
2 Holy Trinity Church
3 Chelsea Royal Hospital
4 Oscar Wilde Home: 44 Tite St.
5 Oscar Wilde Home: 34 Tite St.
6 Chelsea Physic Garden
7 Chelsea Embankment
8 3 Cheyne Walk
9 George Eliot Home: 4 Cheyne Walk
10 Bertrand Russell Home:
   14 Cheyne Walk
11 Dante Gabriel Rossetti Home: No. 16
   Cheyne Walk
12 Henry VIII Home: 19-26 Cheyne Walk
13 48 Cheyne Walk
14 Carlyle Mansions
15 Elizabeth Gaskell Home:
   93 Cheyne Walk

16 Brunel Home: 98 Cheyne Walk
17 James Abbott McNeill Whistler
   Home: 101 Cheyne Walk
18 Hilarie Belloc Home:
   104 Cheyne Walk
19 J.M.W. Turner Home:
   119 Cheyne Walk
20 Granny Takes a Trip
21 World's End
22 Apple Tailoring
23 Chelsea Potter
24 The Pheasantry
25 Bazaar
26 Chelsea Drugstore
27 Saatchi Gallery

Round Pond

Hyde Park

The Serpentine

Kensington
Gardens

Hyde Park
Tennis Centre

N

London

Royal
College
of Art

Kensington Rd

Knightsbridge

Knightsbridge

Belgrave
Square

Ennismore
Gardens

Belgrave Pl

Royal College
of Music

Exhibition Rd

Brompton Rd

Cadogan Place
Gardens

Chesham Pl
Eaton Pl

Lyall St

Queen's Gate

Beauchamp Pl

Pont St

1

Sloane St

Chesham Pl

Chesham St

Science
Museum

Cromwell Gardens

Brompton

Lennox
Gardens

Cadogan
Square
Gardens

Belgravia

Natural History
Museum

Queen's
Gate
Gardens

Cromwell Rd

South Kensington

Eaton Gate

Gloucester Rd

Thurloe St

2

Old Bromton Rd

South Kensington

Sloane
Square

Sloane Ave

Draycott Pl

King's Rd

Lower Sloane St

Pimlico Rd

Holy Trinity
Brompton

27

Chelsea

Onslow
Gardens

St. Lukes Church

25

26

Chelsea Bridge Rd

Boltons

Royal
Brompton
Hospital

St. Luke's
Gardens

24

Royal Hospital Rd

Bourton
Court

Elm Park
Gardens

Fulham Rd

Old Church St

23

Radnor Walk

Flood St

3

Ranelagh
Gardens

22

Chelsea Old
Town Hall

King's Rd

Oakley St

Tite St

5

4

Chelsea and
Westminster
Hospital

8

6

Langton St

10

9

Chelsea
Physic Garden

Chelsea Embankment

12

11

7

Edith Grove

21

14

13

Cheyne Walk

Albert Bridge

River Thames

17

15

Millman St

18

16

20

Chelsea
Theatre

19

Battersea Bridge

Albert Bridge Rd

Battersea Park

Cremorne Rd

Battersea Bridge Rd

Duck

1000 ft

200 m

Ladies Pond

Boating
Lake

START:
Sloane Street

TUBE:
▬ Knightsbridge

END:
Sloane Square

TUBE:
▬▬ ▬ Sloane Square

Oscar Wilde

Cheyne Walk in Chelsea circa 1800. Chelsea Old Church is in the distance.

Sloane Street and King's Road are streets closely associated with some of London's most extreme native fashions, though the looks locals have created over the decades couldn't be more divergent. Sloane Street is spiritual home—and in some cases the actual home—of the "Sloane Rangers," the wealthy young women (and some men) who dress, speak and shop identically. (At one time, the young Lady Diana Spencer was dubbed "Supersloane" by style journalists, in gentle satire.) King's Road, on the other hand, was the central artery of Swinging London and the birthplace of the punk rock look. In between the two, stately homes have housed everyone from Oscar Wilde to Keith Richards.

1 Besides its (very) expensive shops, Sloane Street has a couple of other notable attractions. One is the elegant Cadogan Hotel, to your right at No. 75; a blue plaque commemorates that actress Lillie

Langtry once lived here. This is also where Oscar Wilde was arrested for "committing acts of gross indecency with other male persons," in Room 118, on April 6, 1895; in 1937 the future Poet Laureate John Betjeman wrote a simple but touching poem about the incident, "The Arrest of Oscar Wilde at the Cadogan Hotel."

2 On the left is the Holy Trinity Church, a fine Arts and Crafts style building; John Betjeman wrote a poem about it in the 1940s and led a campaign to save it from demolition in the 1970s.

Statue of Sir John Betjeman at St. Pancras station

3 Keep going in the same direction onto Lower Sloane Street and turn right onto Royal Hospital Road, where you will find the Royal Hospital Chelsea, commissioned by Charles II as a home for his injured and discharged soldiers. Constructed from 1682 to 1692, it is a fine example of the work of architect Sir Christopher Wren. It still performs its original function: About 450 retired soldiers, the famous red-jacketed "Chelsea pensioners," enjoy its amenities today.

4 Turn left on Tite Street. The Irish writer Oscar Wilde called Chelsea home for most of his London years, first at 44 Tite Street.

Royal Hospital and Rotunda, by Thomas Bowles, 1750s

Lillie Langtry
Born on the island of Jersey in 1853, actress Lillie Langtry entered London society at 20 through her marriage to Irish landowner Edward Langtry. The beauty soon became friends with the city's elite, including Oscar Wilde and actress Sandra Bernhardt, who suggested she try acting. Langtry made her debut in 1881 at the Haymarket Theatre in *She Stoops to Conquer*. This lead to tours of the U.S., where she eventually became a citizen. Langtry's personal conquests are nearly as celebrated as her triumphs on the stage. Among them: a three-year affair with the future king, Edward VII, then married with six children. The home he built for her is now a boutique country hotel called Langtry Manor.

Cheyne Walk, 1881

5 And then, from 1884 to the year of his downfall, Wilde lived at No. 34. The latter house was thoroughly redecorated in accordance with Wilde's aesthetic theories—lots of white, primrose, yellow and blue, with painted dragons and peacock tails. It was here he penned his renowned works *The Picture of Dorian Grey* and *The Importance of Being Earnest*. You can spot it by the blue memorial plaque on the wall.

6 Return to Royal Hospital Road and make a left. Continue to the Chelsea Physic Garden at Swan Walk, which was originally (from 1673) a medical institution, devoted to research into the curative properties of plants by the Society of Apothecaries.

7 Royal Hospital Road intersects with the Chelsea Embankment, which offers views across the river to Battersea, and which then runs into Cheyne Walk. Part of the walk stands on the ground that was once occupied by the manor house built by Sir Thomas More in 1523; it was confiscated by the king in 1534. Cheyne Walk is not merely saturated with historical associations, but is one of the most handsome streets in London, with the River Thames on one side and some very fine houses—some Jacobean—on the other.

8 The roll call of other Cheyne Walk residents includes writers, royals and two Rolling Stones. Guitarist Keith Richards and his girlfriend Anita Pallenberg lived together at No. 3. Before guitarist Steve Jones formed the Sex Pistols, he broke into Richards's home and stole a television.

9 The novelist George Eliot lived at No.4; she died here in 1880.

10 Philosopher Bertrand Russell lived at No. 14 while writing *The Principles of Mathematics*.

11 Dante Gabriel Rossetti, co-founder of the Pre-Raphaelite Brotherhood, moved into No.16 after the death of his beautiful and beloved wife, Elizabeth Siddal, in 1862, and converted it into a world of his own. It swarmed with his large and exotic collection of animals, including a bull, a zebra, a donkey, several wombats, an armadillo, a kangaroo, assorted lizards, a raccoon, an opossum, a raven and many peacocks, which made a hideous racket. Other human inhabitants of Rossetti's private kingdom included the novelist George Meredith and the poet Algernon Charles Swinburne.

Dante Gabriel Rossetti (left) and family, photographed by Lewis Carroll

Elizabeth Siddal And Dante Gabriel Rossetti

A familiar face peers out again and again from the canvases of the English painters known as the Pre-Raphaelites, pale and surrounded by a mane of red hair. Her name was Elizabeth Siddal.

Born in 1829, Siddall (she would later shorten her surname) was working in a hat shop when the young artist Walter Deverell asked if she'd model for him. Deverell's teacher, Dante Gabriel Rossetti, was impressed and she soon became a favorite subject of the Pre-Raphaelite Brotherhood, a group motivated by a shared love of the Renaissance. Her famous face, no doubt idealized, can be seen in such masterpieces as John Everett Millais's *Ophelia*, for which she posed in a cold bath for hours.

Siddal and Rossetti became lovers and lived together on Chatham Place, but did not marry until 1860. By then, their relationship had grown strained; Rossetti was seeing another model, Jane Burden, and Siddal retreated into opium addiction. The next year, after the birth of a stillborn daughter, Siddal died of an overdose of laudanum, liquid opium, at 32. Rossetti was grief-stricken; he buried his wife with a copy of his poetry and painted *Beata Beatrix* in memorial. But death isn't the end of Siddal's sad story.

By 1869, Rossetti had fallen out of favor. Looking for a new masterpiece, he recalled the poems he had buried with Siddal, and ordered her coffin exhumed. According to legend, when the casket was opened, Siddal's body remained perfectly preserved; her fiery red hair had grown to fill the coffin. Rossetti published his poems, but they were a flop. He too fell into laudanum addiction, attempting suicide in 1872. He survived and went on to live until 1882, never to match his early success.

12 King Henry VIII's Manor House once occupied the site now occupied by numbers 19-26.

13 Mick Jagger lived with girlfriend Marianne Faithfull at No. 48.

14 Henry James and T.S. Eliot lived in Carlyle Mansions, an apartment building at No. 21. Ian Fleming moved here in the early 1950s; his childhood home was No. 119.

Old Church

15 Novelist Elizabeth Gaskell was born at No. 93 in 1810.

16 The Lindsey House, which spans Nos. 96 to 101 was home to two giants of British engineering, Marc Brunel and his son, Isambard Kingdom Brunel (who lived in No. 98). The younger Brunel would go on to become more famous than his father, building the Great Western Railway.

17 The great American painter James Abbott McNeill Whistler lived at No. 101 for three years (1863-66), venturing out to paint many pioneering studies of the river's docks and warehouses. He then moved to No. 96 (1866-1878) where he painted, among other subjects, his single most famous work, a portrait of his mother. He adorned this home with Japanese fans and wall-hangings, and he slept on a large Chinese bed.

Arrangement in Grey and Black No.1 (Whistler's Mother), 1871

Then & Now

Lindsey House

18 The Catholic writer and politician Hilaire Belloc lived at No.104.

19 The picturesque walk has been a magnet for writers and painters alike, including J.M.W. Turner, who lived at No. 119 with his mistress, Sophia Booth, until his death in 1851, under the alias "Mr. Booth." Ian Fleming, the creator of James Bond, lived here in his teens and twenties.

J.M.W. Turner, by John Linnell, 1838

After Cheyne Walk, take a right onto Milman's Street and walk a little to the north until you meet King's Road, originally built for King Charles II as a private way. In the 1960s, it was the crown jewel of "Swinging London," a place for fashion stores, clubs, restaurants, and other playgrounds of the young, groovy and rich. King's Road gained its association with fashion in 1955, when the designer Mary Quant opened the very first so-called boutique, Bazaar, at 138a. Musicians from around the world also gathered here; the Beatles debuted *Sgt. Pepper's* from the windows of Mama Cass's flat near here. Most of the places from the Swinging Era have since closed or changed their character.

20 At No. 488 King's Road was Granny Takes a Trip, one of the most famous clothes stores of the day, run by the entrepreneur Nigel Waymouth and opened in 1966. The air reeked with patchouli oil, rock and pop music throbbed from the speakers, and the satin jackets, crushed velvet loon pants and kaftans flew out the door. Its storefront façade went through many artistic incarnations, from giant portraits of Native American chiefs and Jean Harlow to a '48 Dodge saloon car that appeared to be crashing out through the front window. The store closed in 1974. Novelist Salman Rushdie lived in the upstairs flat for a while.

Granny Takes a Trip, 1967

21 Nostalgists longing for a slightly more recent phase of youth rebellion should also visit No. 430, which has gone under many names: Hung On You, Mr. Freedom and, from 1971 to 1972, when it was run by Malcolm McLaren and Vivienne Westwood, Let It Rock, a clothing store which specialized in the look of the 1950s Teddy Boys. Restless with both names and styles, the couple renamed it Too Fast To Live, Too Young To Die in 1972, and in 1974 renamed it again as SEX, with a line in rubber and other fetishistic clothing. It was in the SEX period that McLaren took up the Sex Pistols, and in 1976 the store morphed yet again into Seditionaries. By the 1980s, Westwood had become an influential fashion designer and she rebranded No. 430 under the title it still holds today, World's End.

Malcolm McLaren and
Vivienne Westwood, 1977

22 At No.161, Apple Tailoring, owned by the Beatles' company, sold clothes for a short time.

23 The Chelsea Potter (Nos. 117-119) was a favorite pub for hot new actors, including Michael Caine and Terence Stamp.

24 At No. 152, The Pheasantry operated a glamorous restaurant and night club; when the club was closed down, that section of the building was converted into flats, and one of the early tenants was Eric Clapton; today it houses a pizza restaurant.

25 Mary Quant, credited with creating the mod mini skirt, hot pants, sweater dresses and brightly colored stockings, presided over Bazaar at No. 138a.

26 The building at No. 49 was a combined shopping center, restaurant and disco: The Chelsea Drugstore, as mentioned in the Rolling Stones' song "You Can't Always Get What You Want." Groovy.

27 Continue along King's Road. On your right, in the Duke of York's Headquarters, is the Saatchi Gallery. One of the world's leading contemporary art galleries, it is more of a museum than gallery, and will soon become the Museum of Contemporary Art, London thanks to a donation from gallery owner Charles Saatchi. The gallery opened in 1985 as a place to exhibit the fine-art collection of the advertising executive, a champion of Damien Hirst, Tracey Emin and the Young British Artists that emerged in the late 1980s. Since 2008, its massive 70,000-square-foot space has been home to a number of galleries featuring rotating exhibitions showcasing new art from China, Germany and Russia, as well as a bookshop and café.

At the end of King's Road you will return to Sloane Square and the Sloane Square station on the Circle and District lines.

Then & Now

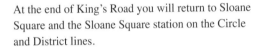

Top: Mary Quant at Bazaar. 138A King's Rd.
Bottom: The Chelsea Drugstore, c. 1970, 26-1. 49 King's Rd.

WESTMINSTER

N

London

rook St
or St.
Maddox St.
Berkeley Square
een Park
Piccadilly
een Square
Constitution Hill
gham Gardens

Maddox St.
arnaby St
Lexington St
St Anne Church
Covent Garden
Golden Square
Brewer St
Shaftesbury Ave
Rupert St
Leicester Square
Air St
Trocadero
Leicester Square
Piccadilly Circus
Orange St
Charing Cross
Jermyn St
Regent St
Charing Cross
14
St. James's St
King St
St. James's Square
Pall Mall
16
15
Whitehall
Embankment
13
18
The Mall
17
Horse Guards Rd
12
11
Parliament St
9
10
8
Victoria Embankment
6
Queen Victoria Memorial
St. James's Park
5
7
Westminster
Great George St
Bridge St
19
Birdcage Walk
St.James's Park
4
3
Westminster Bridge
Abingdon St
Waterloo Bridge
London Eye
Jubilee Gardens
River Thames
St. Thomas Hospital
Lambeth Palace Rd
Archbishop's Park
ingham Palace Rd
Bressenden Pl
Victoria St
Greycoat Pl
Victoria Tower Gardens
Wilton Rd
Victoria
Horseferry Rd
Westminster Hospital
Millbank
Lambeth Bridge
Lambeth Rd
Vincent Square
Belgrave Rd
Vauxhall Bridge Rd
Albert Embankment
Black Prince Rd
ccleston Sq
2
St. George's Dr
Pimlico
Grosvenor Rd
Sutherland St
Lupus St
Vauxhall Bridge
1
Vauxhall
Kennington Ln
Vauxhall

1000 ft
200 m

START:
Intersection of Millbank
and Vauxhall Bridge Road

TUBE:
▬ Pimlico

END:
Buckingham Palace

TUBE:
▬ ▬ Victoria
▬

This classic tourist walk takes in London's major centers of political, administrative, royal, military, spiritual and even artistic power. Not all of the places listed here are necessarily fine architecture—some people hate the Gothic Revival style of the Palace of Westminster, others think it magnificent—but almost every building, ancient as Westminster Abbey or modern as the MI6 building, has played a part in the narrative of London, and of the United Kingdom.

Start from Pimlico Underground station, or, if you prefer, from the intersection of Millbank and Vauxhall Bridge Road.

1 Straight across from Millbank on the south bank of the Thames is the MI6 Building, a startling piece of architectural fantasy designed by Terry Farrell, sometimes known as the Aztec Temple or Babylon-on-Thames. It was completed in 1994, after a murky interlude when the British Government was not admitting to the existence of the secret service agency that is now based there. It will be familiar to anyone who has seen the James Bond film *The World Is Not Enough*, in which it appears to be blown up by terrorists. A perpetual question: Why is a *secret* service housed in such a glaringly conspicuous building?

2 Head due north along Millbank until you reach Tate Britain, formerly known as the Tate Gallery until its holdings of international art were shipped up the river and found a new home in the huge Tate Modern. (See Tour 9, the Southwark walk.) It contains probably the best collection of British art anywhere in the world, including a wonderful gathering of paintings by Joseph Mallord William Turner in the Clore Gallery. There is something here to please almost everyone: William Hogarth, William Blake, John Constable, John Martin, the Pre-Raphaelites. Tate Britain also has one of the best restaurants in London (the Rex Whistler), with possibly the best décor: a giant mural by the artist of the same name.

3 Carry on north up Millbank, past the Victoria Tower Gardens, until you reach the complex of the Palace of Westminster, made up of the Houses of Parliament and Westminster Hall, plus the clock tower which houses the giant bell known as Big Ben. (Pedants insist that it is only the bell, and not the clock or clock tower, that has the right to that nickname; almost everyone calls the tower Big Ben anyway.) Many people think that it is a very old building; in fact, most of the old Westminster Palace, a rather ramshackle place, burned down in 1834, leaving only Westminster Hall and a few other parts intact. The new Palace was built by a brilliant duo, Charles Barry and Augustus Pugin, from 1835-1860.

The Palace of Westminster from the River after the Fire of 1834, by an unknown artist c. 1834

The Coronation Banquet of King George IV in Westminster Hall, 1821

Sir Thomas More, by Hans Holbein the Younger, 1527

Before the Palace was a home to Britain's democratically elected governments, it was a home for monarchs. The area, known as "Thorney Island," may well have been used as a residence by King Cnut. The original Westminster Palace was built here at the behest of Edward the Confessor, at roughly the same time that Westminster Abbey was first constructed; very little of that early structure survives. The Palace became the principal home of kings until Henry VIII moved to Whitehall Palace. The Curia Regis, an early form of Parliament, would meet at Westminster, and was followed from 1295 onwards by a succession of later types of Parliament.

Apart from the Jewel Tower, which used to house the Crown Jewels that are now held in the Tower of London, the only major part of the Palace to have escaped the fire of 1834 is Westminster Hall, a magnificent piece of medieval architecture that has also been the site of some great political dramas. Richard II, who ordered the elaborate

Then & Now

Houses of Parliament, Effect of Fog, by Claude Monet, 1890. Metropolitan Museum of Art

carpentry of the roof, was later deposed under that same woodwork. Among those tried and sentenced to death here: William Wallace (1305), Sir Thomas More (1535), Guy Fawkes (1606) and Charles I (1649).

4 Almost immediately next to Britain's home of secular power, just past the church of St. Margaret, is its most cherished home of sacred power, Westminster Abbey, a UNESCO World Heritage Site. There have been a total of sixteen royal weddings held here, including Prince William and Kate Middleton's marriage, held in April 2011.

5 When you have had your fill of these sights— look out for the statues of various leading characters in this book, including Richard the Lionheart, Oliver Cromwell and Winston Churchill—re-orient yourself and head north from Parliament Square and onto the street known as Whitehall, which is also the name for this compact district and a synonym for the British Government. First on the left is the Treasury which has charge of the nation's economy, and also plays home to the Churchill War Rooms. At the start of the Second World War, the British Government set up an emergency base deep beneath the Treasury, and shielded it from bomb attacks with a thick layer of concrete. It was from this complex that Churchill ran the war campaign from December 1940 onwards. It has been open to the public as a museum since 1984.

6 Next on the left, after King Charles Street, is the Foreign and Commonwealth Office. It is located in a building (constructed from 1861-68) designed by George Gilbert Scott in an Italianate style at the insistence of Lord Palmerston, then Prime Minister.

Russian President Vladimir Putin and British Prime Minister Tony Blair in 2000

7 Opposite the FCO, and in the middle of the road, is the Cenotaph, Britain's national monument to the war dead. Designed by the great architect Edward Lutyens in 1919, it was originally a wood-and-plaster structure. The permanent Portland stone structure was built, using Lutyens's design, between 1919 and 1920. Every year, on the Sunday closest to November 11, Armistice Day, a ceremony is held here, heavily attended by veterans. The Monarch lays a wreath of poppies, and there is silence. It is intensely moving.

8 On the left is the entrance to Downing Street, which was built in 1682 by Sir George Downing—who, by the way, was the second person to graduate from Harvard University. It has been a tradition (though not a rule) for British Prime Ministers to have their main London home here at No. 10, ever since Sir Robert Walpole—the first politician to take that title—took up residence in 1732. The Chancellor of the Exchequer lives at No. 11. Interesting fact: The first inhabitant of No. 10 was Sir Thomas Knyvet, the Justice of the Peace who arrested Guy Fawkes. Downing Street used to be open to the public, but railings were put up at the ends of the street in the 1980s to thwart latter-day followers of Guy Fawkes.

9 To the immediate north of Downing Street, at 70 Whitehall, is the Cabinet Office, which stands on a site where Henry VIII used to play tennis—remains of this tennis court can be seen within the building.

10 On the other side of the road is a large, undistinguished building, constructed between 1938 and 1959 in twentieth-century neoclassical style: the headquarters of the Ministry of Defense.

Old Horse Guards and the Banqueting Hall, Whitehall from St. James's Park by Canaletto, 1749

Whitehall Palace

Contemporary German print depicting Charles I's beheading, 1649

11 Part of the ground on which the MOD stands is occupied by the Banqueting House, often neglected by tourists but a fascinating place. This is the only surviving part of the (mainly) sixteenth-century Whitehall Palace that remains intact above ground—though the wine cellars are preserved underneath the MOD.

Whitehall Palace grew out of an earlier building, York Place, which was the London home of the Archbishop of York. Henry VIII seized it from Cardinal Wolsey in 1529 and developed it into a grand 2,000-room palace, plus bowling greens, tennis courts and a cockpit.

The Banqueting House was designed by Inigo Jones and built from 1619-22, at the orders of James I, and was the first building in the country to have been built in an Italianate Renaissance style that later became fashionable. There is a remarkable ceiling painting, by Peter Paul Rubens, which shows James I being welcomed into heaven; it was under this painting that Charles I had to walk when he was led to his execution in 1649.

Horse Guards Parade

Lifeguard

Blues

After the Restoration, Charles II moved in and made it a place of wild debaucheries. The Palace caught fire in 1698, after a washerwoman tried to dry her clothes over a charcoal stove. Christopher Wren drew up plans for a magnificent replacement, but the hypochondriac William III feared damp air and did not fancy living so close to the Thames, so he moved to the building now known as Kensington Palace.

12 Opposite the Banqueting House is one of London's most familiar and pleasing sights: the entrance to Horse Guards Parade, where members of the Household Cavalry—the Life Guards and the Blues & Royals—stand mounted guard on their splendid black horses. The Life Guards (the oldest regiment in the British Army; it began as a personal guard for Charles II during the Interregnum) are the ones in red tunics, with white plumes on their helmets; the Blues wear the obvious color, with red plumes.

13 The final samples of architecture worth a detailed look are the Admiralty Buildings, which date from the early eighteenth century; look out for Robert Adam's Admiralty Screen (1788).

14 Looking towards Trafalgar Square, make a left and pass under Admiralty Arch into The Mall.

15 On the right is the discreet entrance to the ICA, the Institute of Contemporary Arts: a combined cinema, exhibition space and performance area, steadfastly dedicated to the avant-garde and, at one time, notorious for the kind of exhibitions that would have Members of Parliament angrily shouting to have the place closed down.

16 Just beyond the ICA and up a steep flight of steps—by Robert Adam—is the Duke of York Column, a monument to the second son of George III, and commander-in-chief of the British forces at Waterloo. He is the leading candidate as the inspiration for the Grand Old Duke of York, who, as the nursery rhyme has it, "had ten thousand men…"

17 Enjoy your stroll down The Mall, which manages to be uplifting even in bad weather, and perhaps digress into St. James's Park to your left. There is a very fine eastwards view of the Admiralty buildings from the footbridge over the small lake; today, those buildings are framed from behind by the London Eye.

18 Further along The Mall on the right is St. James's Palace, which—surprisingly—is still the official residence of the Sovereign, even though George III moved his court to Buckingham Palace in 1762. Henry VIII had it built between 1531 and 1536. Mary Tudor lived here; Elizabeth I was here at the

Left: *A View of St. James's Palace, Pall Mall* by Thomas Bowles, 1763;
Right: Princess Mary Tudor, detail from a painting by the artist Mabuse, c. 1516

Buckingham House 1710

Buckingham Palace Grand
Staircase 1870

time of the Spanish Armada. Various members of
the royal family and their staffs still reside here.

19 At the end of The Mall is Buckingham Palace,
the traditional—though not the only—London
home for generations of monarchs: George III and
IV; William IV; Victoria (though she neglected the
place for many years, preferring Windsor Castle
or her modest homes on the Isle of Wight and,
above all, in the Scottish Highlands, at Balmoral);
Edward VII and the short-reigning Edward VIII;
George V and VI; and, since 1952, Elizabeth II. As
its name suggests, Buckingham Palace—originally
Buckingham House, or "Buck House"—was built
for the Duke of Buckingham. George III paid its
occupant, the Earl of Arlington, £28,000 for the
place, and installed Queen Charlotte there.

The architectural core of the Palace was designed
by William Winde in 1703. It underwent major
reconstruction in the nineteenth century, mostly
by John Nash and Edward Blore, who elaborated
it into its present basic form of three wings around
a courtyard. Additional alterations in the late
nineteenth and early twentieth centuries added the
famous balcony from which the Queen greets her
subjects. The Palace was bombed several times
in World War II; one German bomb destroyed
the chapel, which was rebuilt as the Queen's
Gallery, where the public can see pictures from Her
Majesty's collections.

Is the flag flying over Buckingham Palace? If so, the
Queen is in residence.

Continue along Buckingham Palace Road to reach
the Victoria Underground station, serviced by the
Circle, District and Victoria lines.

1. *The Painter and his Pug*, by William Hogarth, 1745; **2.** *The Cholmondeley Ladies*, c. 1600-10; **3.** *Norham Castle, Sunrise*, by J.M.W. Turner, c. 1845; **4.** *Ophelia*, by Sir John Everett Millais, 1851-52; **5.** *The Lady of Shalott*, by John William Waterhouse, 1888
6. *Nocturne: Blue and Gold—Old Battersea Bridge*, by James McNeill Whistler, 1872-75
7. *Beata Beatrix*, by Dante Gabriel Rossetti, 1872
8. *Self Portrait*, by J.M.W. Turner, 1799

STRAND AND COVENT GARDEN

N

London

Russell Square

Southampton Row

Bloomsbury

Theobald's Rd

Gray's Inn Gardens

The British Museum

Bedford Square

Bloomsbury St

High Holborn

Chancery Lane

New Oxford St

Tottenham Court Rd

High Holborn

Holborn

26

Newton St

Kingsway

24

Lincoln's Inn Fields

25

Charing Cross Rd

Parker St

Chancery Ln

Fetter Ln

Greek St

Shaftesberry Ave

Endell St

Wild St

Portugal St

Carey St

Holborn

Fleet St

Drury Ln

23

St. Clement

Covent Garden

Bow St

Aldwych

22

Monmouth St

Long Acre

Floral St

16

Inner Temple Gardens

Leicester Square

King St

15

13

17

18

21

Bedford St

14

Maiden Ln

Strand

Temple

St

1

2

12

19

20

Savoy St

Chandos Pl

11

Orange St

3

8

John Adam St

10

River Thames

omb St

5

4

9

Charing Cross

6

Strand

7

Charing Cross

Bernie Spain Gardens

Charing Cross

Northumberland Ave

Embankment

Waterloo Bridge

Waterloo Rd

The Mall

Whitehall

Hungerford Bridge

Stamford St

Horse Guards Rd

Parliament St

Victoria Embankment

London Eye

Waterloo E

York Rd

Jubilee Gardens

Waterloo

Waterloo

Waterloo Rd

Waterloo Station

The Cut

Westminster

Great George St

Big Ben

Westminster Bridge

Baylis Rd

Bridge St

Addinton St

St.Thomas' Hospital

1000 ft

200 m

START:
Leicester Square

TUBE:
▬▬ ▬▬ Leicester Square

END:
Sir John Soane's Museum

TUBE:
▬▬ ▬▬ Holborn

The Strand, looking east from Exeter Change, c. 1824

A walk along the Strand to Covent Garden passes through much of London's cultural history, from grand theaters to literary haunts. It is also home to hallowed halls of academia and law, the London School of Economics and the Inns of Court.

✽

Exit the Underground at Leicester Square (Northern and Piccadilly lines).

1 Start your walk at the Shakespeare statue, located in the middle of the public garden space in Leicester Square. You can impress friends and strangers alike by knowing that the words on Shakespeare's scroll are "There is no darkness but ignorance," a line from his comedy *Twelfth Night*. Fittingly, almost no one knows this fact. Leicester Square, which seethes with tourists at all times of the year, is now best known for its cinemas, including a couple that have the last remaining properly large screens in the capital. Film premieres are held here quite frequently, so there is a decent chance that you will bump into a crowd of paparazzi flashing bulbs at the stars. The square, which was created by the Earl of Leicester (pronounced, roughly: Lester) in the early seventeenth century, has an interesting history, few traces of which remain. Two of England's greatest painters, William Hogarth and Joseph Mallord William Turner, lived and worked here.

2 Leave the Square by either the northeast or the southeast side and have a quick look around Charing Cross Road, which used to be a paradise for second-hand book hunters. Some bookshops have survived, but many have been driven out by the high rents; today, the richest collection of bookshops in the area is in Cecil Court, which runs from the eastern side of the road.

3 When you are done with book browsing, head south towards Trafalgar Square: You will almost immediately see, on the right-hand (or west) side of the road, the National Portrait Gallery. It is one of the few art galleries in the world that can appease visitors who have little or no interest in paintings and sculpture, simply because of its astonishing range of characters, from kings to comedians.

4 Go across the road for a while and visit the exceptionally beautiful church of St. Martin-in-the-Fields. Although the earliest references to the church were in 1222, King Henry VIII had it rebuilt (at the time, the church was literally in the fields between Westminster and London) to house plague victims so they wouldn't have to pass through Whitehall Palace. A new church was later designed by architect James Gibbs and built between 1722–24.

The "Chandos" portrait of William Shakespeare, c. 1600-10

The Three Brontë Sisters (detail), in a 1834 painting by their brother Patrick Branwell. From left to right: Anne, Emily and Charlotte.

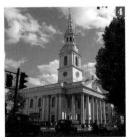

Trafalgar Square

5 Walk just a little farther south, turn right and you are at the entrance to the National Gallery (main structure: William Wilkins, 1832-38). Housing one of the world's finest collections of European art, the Gallery boasts works created between the thirteenth and nineteenth centuries by the likes of Jan van Eyck, Diego Velázquez and Claude Monet.

6 Now it is time to tackle Trafalgar Square, a public space as famous as Piccadilly Circus and—one could argue—much more important to London's life. Londoners gather here every New Year's Eve to drink, make merry and splash in the fountains, which were designed by Sir Edwin Lutyens and built between 1937–39. Crowds also gather here for great national occasions, such as VE Day, or to protest, as in the Poll Tax Riots of 1990. Most of the Square was completed in 1845 to the design of architect Sir Charles Barry, who also rebuilt the Palace of Westminster. From upon its giant column, a statue of Admiral Horatio Nelson (who led the British Royal Navy to a decisive victory during the

Then & Now

Charing Cross Station

Napoleonic Wars and was mortally wounded during the battle) peers down upon the square.

7 Make a left and head east towards Charing Cross Station—not far from the Hungerford Stairs, where Charles Dickens worked in a factory as a child—and the start of the Strand. In the eighteenth century, the buildings along the strand, mainly mansions, were very elegant indeed, and Dr. Samuel Johnson spoke of the street as a place where one could see all of the city's vibrant activities to best advantage. In the nineteenth century, when the mansions gave way to the big railway station, big hotels (the Savoy, the Cecil) and so on, Prime Minister Benjamin Disraeli said that it was one of the finest streets in Europe.

Benjamin Disraeli

8 Its glamour is somewhat faded today, but there is at least one very good modern development— the exclusive Coutts Bank, with its elegant atrium, at No. 440.

9 To the right side of the Strand is a small district of ornate streets and old alleyways, known as Adelphi. It was once a riverside development by the Adam brothers, much of which was destroyed in the 1930s.

10 There is a very striking office block that was built soon after the demolition. At No. 8 John Adam Street is the RSA (Royal Society for the encouragement of Arts, Manufactures and Commerce), an interesting part of which can also be glimpsed from the Strand. Established in 1754, the Royal Society of Arts, as it is commonly referred to, has counted Benjamin Franklin, Stephen Hawking and Karl Marx among its many eminent Fellows; today there are more than 27,000 Fellows in 70 countries worldwide. The Society was one of the main bodies that set up the Festival of Britain in 1951.

11 The Shell Mex House at No. 80 retains the façade of the Cecil Hotel, which was the largest and one of the most glamorous in Europe when it opened in 1896.

12 The oldest restaurant in London, Rules, is nearby, to the left of the Strand in Covent Garden; to reach it, go up Southampton Street and turn left into Maiden Lane. Established in 1798, it serves traditional English game, pies and puddings. The restaurant is particularly enjoyable on a cold winter's evening, when the lights show off its décor to comforting, Dickensian effect. And, yes, Charles Dickens ate here.

13 Back on Southampton Street, turn left to the Covent Garden Market—once the main open space in central London where fruit, vegetables and flowers were sold. (The market moved out in 1974, south of the Thames, to Nine Elms.) Since its re-development and re-opening in 1980, it has been the home to all manner of pubs, cafés, restaurants and craft shops; also to many other kinds of shop, some reasonably cheap, others frighteningly pricey. Street performers provide entertainment that costs as much or as little as you care to tip them.

14 St. Paul's Church, to the west, is often referred to as the "Actors' Church," since so many distinguished members of the theatrical profession have worshipped here over the centuries; there are many memorials for entertainers of all kinds, including Vivien Leigh, Noël Coward and Charlie Chaplin. Its design is attributed to Inigo Jones, who was in charge of the development of the Covent Garden piazza area. Work on the church began in 1631, though the original structure was damaged by fire and was restored in 1798, under the supervision of Thomas Hardwick. It was the first major church to be built in London since the Reformation, and it was said to have been inspired by Jones's study of Palladian architecture during his visits to Italy. In literature, it is famous as the place where Professor Henry Higgins first encounters Eliza Doolittle in *Pygmalion*, the source of *My Fair Lady*.

Vivien Leigh in *Gone with the Wind*

Inigo Jones

15 The Royal Opera House, to the east, has stood on its present site since 1732, though fire destroyed the original theater in 1808 and the second in 1857. Today's façade and auditorium date to 1858, though much else in the building was constructed as part of a massive overhaul in the 1990s. The grand auditorium hosts operas in their original languages and also stages ballets. Don't let the name confuse you—the ROH is often referred to simply as Covent Garden.

16 The Theatre Royal, Drury Lane is the fourth theater to have stood on this site since 1663. (The theater actually opens onto Catherine Street; Drury Lane runs along its back.) The genius architect Sir Christopher Wren designed its

second incarnation, which opened in 1674. In the eighteenth century, thanks to the talents of David Garrick, Richard Brinsley Sheridan and others, it became acknowledged as the greatest theater in town. The present building was erected in 1812, and the theater today is owned by Andrew Lloyd Webber's company. It tends to stage light and undemanding fare.

17 At No. 8 Russell Street is Boswells Café, a modest place rendered immortal as the meeting place of the great author and lexicographer Samuel Johnson and the young Scottish man who would eventually be his biographer, James Boswell. The historic encounter took place at seven in the evening on May 16, 1763. Prices are fair.

18 More suitable for the whole family is London Transport Museum, also on the eastern side. It opened in 1980 and was thoroughly updated from 2005-07.

19 Back in the Strand is the Savoy Hotel, probably the best-known hotel in London, with a very impressive list of guests. It was opened in 1889 by the theatrical impresario Richard D'Oyly Carte, using the profits of the musicals he had produced by Gilbert and Sullivan, particularly their hit show *The Mikado*. Like many other buildings in the vicinity, it has been extensively and expensively updated.

20 At No. 100 is Simpsons-in-the-Strand, which has been serving hearty British food since 1904 and is owned by the Savoy Hotel group.

21 A few survivors from the nineteenth century remain in the area, including some fine churches. St. Mary-le-Strand stands literally in the middle of the road on a traffic island and dates from the eighteenth century, though a twelfth-century church occupied the same place.

22 St. Clement Danes, another "island church," is located where the Strand meets Aldwych. The church likely owes its name to the Danish population that settled here by the permission of Alfred the Great; today it is the central church of the Royal Air Force. The old church was rebuilt by Sir Christopher Wren in 1682.

23 Take Aldwych west and turn right into Kingsway. Just off Kingsway to the right is the London School of Economics, founded in the 1890s and on this site since 1902. Its most famous student is not an economist but a musician: Mick Jagger. At one time, the place was a by-word for militant student activism; it is much more sedate nowadays.

24 Further north up Kingsway and leading off to the right are the roads which lead to Lincoln's Inn Fields, a large grassy area that owes its name to the legal institution based here.

25 To the east of the Fields is Lincoln's Inn, one of London's four surviving Inns of Court (the others being the Inner and Middle Temples and Gray's Inn). The Inns of Court are at the heart of the English and Welsh legal system: All barristers receive their training here, hence their close resemblance to Oxford or Cambridge colleges, with their own lecture rooms, libraries, halls and chapels. All four bodies owe their existence to two events in the thirteenth century: a papal bull which prevented anyone in holy orders from teaching common law (rather than canon law), and an edict by Henry III, which declared that law could not be taught within

William Ewart Gladstone

Margaret Thatcher

Portrait of Sir John Soane
by Sir Thomas Lawrence

the walls of the City. Ejected lawyers gradually drifted to the Holborn region as the most convenient place outside the City for access to Westminster Hall. The early history of the Inns is a little hazy, though Lincoln's Inn was in business by the early fifteenth century and may have been founded as early as the thirteenth. One of the oldest surviving structures here is a wall that dates back to 1562. Four of Britain's Prime Ministers have graduated here: William Pitt the Younger, William Ewart Gladstone, Margaret Thatcher and Tony Blair. Prime Minister Benjamin Disraeli was admitted in 1824 but withdrew seven years later.

26 On the north side of the Fields you will find Sir John Soane's Museum, which, despite its modest dimensions, is a thing of wonder that could justify the effort of a trip to London all on its own. The building was designed by the architect Sir John Soane, best known for his work on the Bank of England, who lived here from 1792 until his death in 1837 and amassed the museum's almost insanely eclectic holdings. Among its treasures are two works by Hogarth—the brilliant satirical engraving *The Election* and the "modern moral subject" in eight parts, *The Rake's Progress*—their savagery undimmed by the centuries. And that's only the beginning. Soane's house is crammed with art and antiquities to make visitors wonder, smile and even laugh: the Monk's Parlour; the grotto devoted to Shakespeare; the memorial to his dog ("Alas, poor Fanny!"); the sarcophagus containing Pharoah Seti I; the Breakfast Room with its tiny convex mirrors…it is probably the most idiosyncratic house in London, and certainly one of the most delightful.

Return to Kingsway to reach the Holborn station on the Central and Piccadilly Lines.

1. *Salome with the Head of John the Baptist*, by Caravaggio, c. 1607-10; **2.** *The Arnolfini Portrait*, by Jan van Eyck, 1434; **3.** *The Bathers*, by Paul Cézanne, 1898-95; **4.** *Sunflowers*, by Vincent van Gogh, 1888; **5.** From left: *Tiger in a Tropical Storm*, by Henri Rousseau, 1891; **6.** *Rain, Steam and Speed–The Great Western Railway*, by J.M.W. Turner, 1844; **7.** *Lady Standing at a Virginal*, by Johannes Vermeer, 1670-72; **8.** *The Virgin and Child with St. Anne and St. John the Baptist*, by Leonardo da Vinci c. 1499-1500 or c. 1506-8

SOHO

1 Piccadilly Circus
2 Marquee Club
3 Admiral Duncan
4 Quo Vadis
5 Royalty Theatre
6 Groucho Club
7 French Pub
8 Hazlitt's
9 Mozart Home: 21 Frith St.

10 Bar Italia
11 Ronnie Scott's
12 Kettner's
13 Coach and Horses
14 Casanova Home: 47 Greek St.
15 L'Escargot
16 The Gay Hussar
17 Soho Square

London

Tottenham Court Rd

Berners St

Oxford St

Soho St

Manor House

17
Soho Square Garden

Noel St

Wardour St

Sheraton St

Dean St

16

Manette St

Greek St

Charing Cross Rd

Stacey St

Benwick St

Wardour Mews

d Mews

Livonia St

8

Warwick House

Frith St

15

14

Royalty House

4

Bateman St

Broadwick St

Duck Ln

5

Dean St

9

Moor St

2

11

10

Ingestre Pl

6

Old Compton St

13

Lexington St

3

7

12

Romilly St

Peter St

Brewer St

Shaftesbury Ave

Chinatown

Newport Pl

Great Pulteney St

Dansey Pl

Gerrard St

Leicester Square

Victory House

Birdle Ln

Glasshouse St

Great Windmill St

Rupert St

Lisle St

Leicester St

Leicester Square

The Imperial

Piccadilly Theatre

London Trocadero

Capital Radio

Regent St

1

Piccadilly Circus

250 ft

50 m

Regent St

Jermyn St

START:
Piccadilly Circus

TUBE:
▬▬ ▬▬ Piccadilly Circus

END:
Soho Square

TUBE:
▬▬ ▬▬ Tottenham
Court Road

▬▬ ▬▬ Oxford Circus
▬▬

Night in Soho

Soho is a place for meandering, though a little historical background will add to the enjoyment of a relaxed stroll from pub to club to café. It has long been London's most cosmopolitan neighborhood, and today there are hundreds of places to eat and drink, at prices ranging from unexpectedly cheap to shockingly expensive. Over the last few decades, Soho has become much more chic than in its old days as a Red Light district, thanks to the influx of film production companies—Wardour Street is the unofficial headquarters of the British film industry—music companies and advertising agencies.

1 Piccadilly Circus, despite its modest scale, is often regarded as the unofficial center of London. Its most recognizable feature is the small statue of Eros, put up in 1892 as a memorial to the philanthropic Earl of Shaftesbury, who gives his name to one of the roads that radiates from the circus. Head northeast up Shaftesbury Avenue, home to several of London's leading theaters, and turn left on Wardour Street.

232

Wardour Street used to be the home of shops which sold antiques, both real and (mainly) fake; in books published before WWII, you will find the term "Wardour Street" applied to anything pretending to be older and more grand than it really is. There is almost no trace of that trade, which has been displaced by offices and restaurants.

2 Rock fans will want to make a pilgrimage to No. 90, former home of the Marquee Club, where some of the biggest names of the '60s and '70s played: The Yardbirds, The Who, David Bowie, Led Zeppelin, Pink Floyd, Jimi Hendrix, and the Sex Pistols, plus dozens of almost equally famous artists. The Marquee's first home (until 1964) was a short walk away at 165 Oxford St., but its glory days were at this location from 1964 to 1988. There have been various attempts to revive the Marquee over the years since 1988, but none of them has been notably successful or long-lived.

Old Compton Street

3 Turn right from Wardour Street and head down Old Compton Street, which has come to be known as the capital of Gay London. There are several bars and shops here that cater to an exclusively gay clientele, of which the most famous is the colorful pub Admiral Duncan. Soho has traditionally been an area with an easy-going attitude to sexuality, and the tolerance extends in both directions—provided you treat the locals with appropriate respect, you will usually not be made to feel unwelcome, no matter how overtly heterosexual you may be.

4 Turn left and head northward along Dean Street to Nos. 26–29, where you will find the fashionable restaurant Quo Vadis, founded by Pepino Leoni in 1923 and owned by artist Damien Hirst and chef Marco Pierre White in the 1990s. It was in

Jenny and Karl Marx lived on Dean St. from 1851-1856

233

Left: Royalty Theatre, Dean Street, 1882; Right: Charles Dickens, 1858

this building that Karl Marx and his family lived, crammed into small and uncomfortable quarters that they shared with an Italian immigrant family. Until recently, the owners of the restaurant allowed people to go upstairs and see the place where he plotted the downfall of capitalism.

5 Charles Dickens spent a good deal of time on Dean Street during his early days as an author and used to enjoy a spot of amateur acting at the Royalty Theatre, which used to stand on the site of Nos. 73-74 Dean St. Dickens staged a production of Ben Jonson's *Every Man in his Humour* here in December 1845. It is also said that Lord Nelson spent the night before sailing for Trafalgar on Dean Street, and used some of his time at a nearby undertaker, selecting the coffin he would be buried in should he not survive the battle.

6 At 45 Dean St. is the Groucho Club, a watering hole for those who work in journalism, film, television, advertising and related industries. It takes its name from Groucho Marx's crack that he would never want to belong to any club with standards low enough to admit him. The policy is strictly members and guests only, but you could try bluffing.

7 On the lower part of Dean Street, to the south of Old Compton Street, you will discover a small but highly characterful and much-loved pub: The French Pub or "French House" (or, simply, "The French," i.e. "Let's meet at the French") at No. 49, just a few steps away from the intersection with Romilly Street. It is a little slice of old France in central London. General Charles de Gaulle and other Free French used to drink here during the War, when it was the unofficial HQ of the French Resistance; to this day the barmaids will not serve you beer in a pint glass, only a half-pint. It is often very crowded, but quite apart from its important role in World War II, it is one of the last surviving reminders of Soho's poorer and more bohemian days; some of the older drinkers there can be coaxed into telling stories of the famous drunks. If you don't care much for halves of beer, try the Breton cider. The restaurant upstairs is usually very good.

8 Next, turn left on Romilly Street, to reach Frith Street, which runs parallel with Dean Street. The brilliant English Romantic journalist, painter and essayist William Hazlitt—a man who, among his many other accomplishments, more or less founded the genre of the "celebrity profile" in his book *The Spirit of the Age*—lived and died at No. 6, now the site of a boutique hotel named Hazlitt's in his memory. It was a favorite of the American writer Susan Sontag, who often stayed here.

9 The young Wolfgang Amadeus Mozart lived at 21 Frith St. for over a year during his two-year residence in London, from April 23, 1764 to July 30, 1765. The Mozart family shared modest lodgings with Thomas Williamson, a "staymaker" (manufacturer of corsets). It was during his time in London that Mozart, age nine, wrote his first symphony. The building where he lived was torn down and rebuilt in 1858; a blue plaque commemorates his stay.

10 At No. 22 is the ever-popular Bar Italia, which serves coffee and snacks and never, ever seems to close. In an upstairs room, in October 1925, John Logie Baird made his first successful trial of television equipment; he showed it off to members of the Royal Institution on January 26, 1926.

Mozart lived here with his father and sister while in London during a grand tour of Europe as a child prodigy

Wolfgang Amadeus Mozart, 1763

The Four Times: Noon,
by William Hogarth 1738

Giacomo Casanova 35, 1760

11 On the other side of the street is Britain's best-known jazz club, Ronnie Scott's, which, since it moved here in 1965, has hosted many of the greatest names in jazz.

12 Walk south, past Old Compton Street and make a left on Romilly Street. At the corner with Greek Street is 29 Romilly, an up-market restaurant, Kettner's, once a favourite haunt of Oscar Wilde and the high-living Edward VII. It is still in service as a restaurant, though less grand nowadays than in its Victorian and Edwardian heyday.

13 The building across the road from Kettner's is another of London's most celebrated pubs, the Coach and Horses (just next door is the patisserie shop and café Maison Bertaux, which has been in business since 1871) made immortal in a series of grimly humorous columns in *The Spectator* by the journalist and alcoholic Jeffrey Bernard, and also the home of the famous weekly lunches hosted by the satirical magazine *Private Eye*—an invaluable British institution which, in addition to being very funny, has uncovered some of the major political scandals of the last fifty years. Its legendary landlord, Norman Balon, "the rudest landlord in London," handed over the keys to the place on May 22, 2006, but the sign outside continues to proclaim the pub's alternative name: Norman's.

14 Turn left on Greek Street, the third of the main streets to cut a north/south path through Soho. Suitably enough for a district once noted for its sex industry, Greek Street was also a temporary home for Giacomo Casanova, who lived at No. 47 in 1764 (which makes him a near neighbor of the child Mozart).

15 Even for a district rich in restaurants, Greek Street is unusually well supplied with places to lunch and dine. One of its most famous is L'Escargot at No. 48, which boasts a Michelin star and a price tag to match.

16 Another favorite Greek Street restaurant is the Gay Hussar at No. 2. The Gay Hussar, despite its proximity to Old Compton Street, is not a resort for homosexual cavalrymen, but a vintage Hungarian restaurant that continues to serve traditional, filling foods. Caricatures by Martin Rowson, one of Britain's leading cartoonists, now dominate the walls. Rowson himself can often be found here.

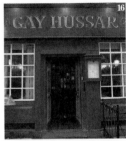

17 Finally, head north into Soho Square, which in fine weather is a pleasant, leafy place to relax on a park bench. In the middle of the square is an incongruously rural sight: a half-timbered gardener's hut. The square dates back to the 1680s, and at one time was one of the most desirable residential districts in London; it has also been home to one of the capital's notorious brothels. Today, various media companies, including one owned by Sir Paul McCartney, dominate the Square. A restored statue of Charles II by Caius Gabriel Cibber has cast a cold eye on passersby ever since it was returned to its traditional site in 1938.

Exit the park north on Soho Street and turn right on Oxford Street to reach the Tottenham Court Road station on the Central and Northern lines. The station is undergoing construction through 2018, so you may choose to turn left instead on Oxford Street and continue to Oxford Circus (Bakerloo, Central and Victoria lines).

BLOOMSBURY

N

London

Mornington
Crescent

St.Pancras
Gardens

Camley St
Natural Park

Robert St

Eversholt St

St.James's
Gardens

Euston

Euston

Ossulston St

Midland Rd

St.Pancras

St.Pancras
International

King's Cross

14

Pentonville Rd

King's Cross Rd

13

12

King's Cross
St.Pancras

Albany St

Euston Rd

Euston Rd

Upper Woburn Pl

Judd St

Tavistock Pl

St.George's
Gardens

Regent Sq

Gray's Inn Rd

Doughty St

Euston Square

11

Gordon
Square

Coram's
Fields

Euston Rd

Warren St

Gower St

Tavistock
Square

4

Russell Square

Guilford St

15

Great
ortland St

Fitzroy
Square

Maple St

Howland St

Torrington Pl

5

3

Russell
Square

Bloomsbury

10

9

Great Clipstone St

8

Cleveland St

7

Goodge St

Goodge St

Berners Mews

6

Charlotte St

Gower St

2

Tottenham Ct Rd

Bedford
Square

Bloomberry St

British
Museum

1

Southampton Row

Theobald's Rd

High Holborn

Horborn

Margaret St

Berners St

Oxford St

Tottenham
Court Rd

New Oxford St

High Holborn

Lincoln's
Inn Fields

Great Portland St

Noel St

Soho
Square

Kingsway

Aldwych

rcus

Prince St

Bridle Ln

St Anne Church

Covent Garden

Maddox St

Regent St

Golden
Square

Shaftesbury Ave

Leicester Square

Strand

Waterloo
Bridge

Piccadilly Circus

Air St

Piccadilly

Jermyn St

1000 ft

200 m

START:
British Museum

TUBE:
▇▇▇ ▬▬ Holborn
▇▇▇ ▬▬ Tottenham Court

END:
Dickens Museum

TUBE:
▬▬▬ Chancery Lane
▇▇▇ ▬▬ Holborn

Fitzroy Tavern

British Musuem, 1852

Rosetta Stone

Bloomsbury—with its large and sometimes graceful squares, university buildings, bookshops, pubs and, dominating the area, the British Museum—and neighboring Fitzrovia were once the center of the city's bohemian literary scene, home to Virginia Woolf, John Maynard Keynes and Authur Rimbaud.
To explore the area, start from Holborn Underground station (you could also use Tottenham Court Road station, though at the time of writing it is undergoing extensive development and some trains do not stop there) then keep going up Southampton Row and turn left onto Great Russell Street.

1 The British Museum grew from a bequest by Sir Hans Sloane in 1753 and was originally devoted to the then-young sciences of biology and geology, as well as medicine and the fine arts. The collection grew enormously over the next hundred years, one major windfall being loot from Egypt—including the Rosetta Stone—brought back after the defeat of Napoleon's forces there in 1801. With eight million artifacts and artworks spanning all of human history, from Afghanistan to Zimbabwe, the museum is the most-visited in England (and the second in the world).

The famous domed and circular Reading Room of the British Library, which opened in 1857, is no more: the Library moved out of the building in 1997 to its new premises in St. Pancras (see 🔢). Leading architecture firm Foster + Partners imaginatively developed the space it occupied into the "Great Court," an airy and well-lit circular structure, two acres large and very handsome indeed.

🔢 To the north of the Museum is the Senate House of the University of London, built in the Art Deco style during the 1930s; some find it stylish, others vaguely fascistic. George Orwell used it as the home of his "Ministry of Truth" in his frightening novel 1984, inspired by the fact that it had been used by the actual Ministry of Information during WWII.

🔢 Thornhaugh Street, which runs between Malet Street and Russell Square, is the home of SOAS: The School of Oriental and African Studies. Founded in 1916 and originally based in Finsbury Circus, SOAS moved to its purpose-built headquarters from 1938 onwards, a process sometimes impeded by German bombs. It was conceived as a place where colonial administrators might be trained, but has developed into a center of scholarship for languages, law, economics, culture and other leading aspects of the regions it studies. Famous early alumni include the American singer Paul Robeson; probably the most celebrated of recent graduates is the Burmese Nobel laureate Aung San Suu Kyi.

4 Continue on to Gordon Square. For literary and artistic types, Bloomsbury invariably summons up images of the Bloomsbury Group of writers, thinkers, sexual experimenters and artists: Virginia Woolf and her husband Leonard, Lytton Strachey, John Maynard Keynes, Vanessa Stephen, Clive Bell and others. Sadly, many of their old haunts and homes were destroyed during the Blitz; the best surviving place for pilgrimage is Gordon Square, where most of them lived at one time or another.

5 Locate at 62-64 Gower St. is the Royal Academy of Dramatic Arts, the UK's best-known training ground for actors. The roll call of those who began their careers here is intimidatingly long and covers many generations, from John Gielgud (who studied here in 1923 and for whom one of the academy's three theaters is named), Charles Laughton and Vivien Leigh, to Peter O'Toole, Roger Moore, Albert Finney, John Hurt and Alan Rickman, to Clive Owen, Ralph Finnes and Kenneth Branagh, to Maggie Gyllenhall and Gemma Arterton.

Dylan Thomas

6 Cross Tottenham Court Road and enter the district sometimes known as "Fitzrovia." At 16 Charlotte St. you will find the Fitzroy Tavern, today most often frequented by students from University College and, from time to time, members of the *Dr. Who* Fan Club. But in the period during and after the war it was one of the great centers of London's literary and artistic bohemia. Dylan Thomas, George Orwell, Anthony Burgess and others all supped pints and whiskeys here, as did the notoriously promiscuous painter Augustus John. It used to be said that when John walked through the streets of Fitzrovia, he would pat the head of every child he passed, just in case it was one of his own.

Augustus John

7 Jack the Ripper conspiracy theorists make pilgrimages to 20 Cleveland St., where they believe Prince Eddy, eldest son of the future Edward VII, fathered an illegitimate child with a shopgirl named Annie Cook, whom he later secretly married. The child was farmed out to Mary Kelly, one of the Ripper's victims. It's still speculated that the Ripper may have been Prince Eddy himself, or possibly the distinguished painter Walter Sickert, rumored to have given Eddy painting lessons nearby.

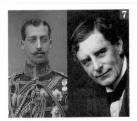

Prince Eddy and Walter Sickert

Maybe. It is certainly true that Eddy was implicated in a notorious scandal that blew up when the police discovered a homosexual brothel operating at 19 Cleveland St. (since demolished and re-numbered as 18).

8 You are now in Fitzrovia, a district often ignored in tourist guides and understandably so: it has no major landmarks except the Telecom Tower (formerly the Post Office Tower), built in the early '60s, when it was by far the city's tallest building.

9 Fitzroy Square is a handsome late-eighteenth century creation badly damaged by the Blitz. Fitzroy Square has become well known to readers of contemporary fiction as the main setting of Ian McEwan's best-selling novel *Saturday*; McEwan is also on the list of writers who have lived in the Square. It was here, at number 33, that the art critic Roger Fry ran his highly influential Omega Workshops during the First World War.

10 No. 29 was successively the home of George Bernard Shaw, who wrote his first two plays here, and, a decade later, of Miss Virginia Stephen, later to be known as Mrs. Virginia Woolf. Woolf lived here from 1907–11.

Virginia Woolf, by George
Charles Beresford, 1902

Beatles memoribilia at the
library's Sir John Ritblat Gallery

To exit the park, make a left onto Grafton Way and continue past Tottenham Court Road to Gower Street, where you will find the Main Building of University College London—UCL facilities are also scattered across Bloomsbury. The main attraction for non-students here is macabre: the mummified body (and wax head) of the philosopher Jeremy Bentham, a rationalist who wished to mock death. He has occasionally been the butt of student pranks.

Next, head north until you meet the Euston Road, turn right (eastwards) and head for the new British Library. Its forecourt is brooded over by a burly statue of Sir Isaac Newton, created by the late Scottish sculptor Eduardo Paolozzi and inspired by an image of Newton painted by William Blake. You must have a library card to use the full resources of the book and journal collections, but there are plenty of attractions for those who just want to browse its open areas and exhibitions, most of which have free admission. The bookshop is large and imaginatively stocked and has a wide selection of works about the history of London.

Now pass St. Pancras Station, much developed in recent years and today the place to catch the Eurostar train to France or Belgium.

The nearby King's Cross Station is undergoing a major redevelopment as this is written. In the *Harry Potter* series the station is the place to catch Hogwarts Express. Unfortunately, only wizards and witches can pass through the brick wall and onto platform 9 ¾.

The Dickens Museum is located a short walk away, at 48 Doughty St. (To reach it from Euston Road, turn right onto Gray's Inn Road, then make a right onto Guilford Street and a left onto Doughty Street.) It has served as a monument to the novelist since it opened in 1925. In fact, Charles Dickens only lived here for a relatively short period of his early career, from 1837 to 1839, but these were months of intense productivity. During his residence he completed his breakthrough work *Pickwick Papers*, completed both *Oliver Twist* and *Nicholas Nickleby*, and began to write *Barnaby Rudge*. The museum holds the most important collection of Dickens papers and editions in the world, as well as assorted memorabilia.

To return to the Undergroud, head back to Gray's Inn Road and head south to Chancery Lane (Central Line). From there turn right on High Holborn to return to the Holborn station on the Piccadilly and Central lines.

The Dickens Museum

MARYLEBONE

South Hampstead

15 Primrose Hill

Wellington
Hospital North

Acacia Rd

Ave Rd

Prince Albert Rd

Outer Cir

14

St.John's Wood

Mornington
Crescent

17

Hell Rd

Wellington Rd

13 Regent's
Park

Robert St

Euston

Euston

St.John's Wood

16

Lisson Grove

Boating Lake

Albany St

Euston Square

Marylebone

Windsor
Castle

Park Square
Gardens

Warren St

Great Portland St

Edgware Rd
(Bakerloo)

Marylebone Flyover

Marylebone Rd

18 Baker Street

19 20 21

Regent's Park

Park Crescent

Portland Pl

Great Portland St

Maple St

Clipstone St

Howland St

Goodge Street

22

Marylebone

Gloucester Pl

Paddington St

Weymouth St

12

Mortimer St

ington

Edgware Rd
(Metropolitan & Circle)

Paddington

Seymour Pl

Crawford St

Baker St

7

8

New Cavendish St

Welbeck St

Wimpole St

10

11 9

Berners St

Noel St

100
Club

Paddington

Sussex Gardens

23

George St

Orchard St

5 Thayer St

6

Wigmore St

Margaret St

St. Johns Church

Edgware Rd

Dulce St

Henrietta Pl

Oxford
Circus

Westbourne
Terrace

Bayswater

Seymour St

2

Bond Street

Prince's St

3

4

Marble Arch

Oxford St

1

Grosvenor
Square

Upper Grosvenor St

Grosvenor St

Regent St

Golden
Square

Brewer St

Lancaster Gate

Bayswater Rd

Cumberland Gate

Mayfair

Piccadilly Circus

The Ring

Park Ln

Park Ln

Hyde
Park

St. James St

Jermyn St

St. Jame's
Square

Green Park

King St

Pall Mall

The Serpentine

Hyde Park Corner

Piccadilly

Green Park

The Mall

Exhibition Rd

Knightsbridge

Constitution Hill

Buckingham
Palace Gardens

Birdcage Walk

Kensington Rd

Knightsbridge

Buckingham
Palace

St.James's Park

1500 ft

300 m

Royal College
of Music

Belgrave
Square

Rock shop on Baker Street

John Nash

Prince Regent

This is a roughly circular route that includes a wander through Regent's Park and ends with a pleasant stroll through Hyde Park. It can be turned into a consumer spree for those who enjoy shopping, but otherwise the mood is more quiet and contemplative than other walks, since only some parts of Marylebone are on the standard routes for visitors. Much of the area's charm is a result from Lambeth-born architect John Nash (1752-1835), whose royal patron the Prince Regent (later George IV) commanded him to create what is now called Regency London, a dramatic swath of historic buildings in an elegantly neo-Classical style.

Begin at the Marble Arch Undergound station on the Central Line.

1 The Marble Arch was originally designed as a grand gateway to Buckingham Palace in 1828, as part of John Nash's overhaul of Buckingham House. It was moved to its present site in 1855. Nash modeled his gateway on the Arch of Constantine in Rome, and ordered huge quantities of marble from Italy for the job. There are a few small rooms inside the arch; it was used as a police station until 1950.

2 Now head westwards into Oxford Street, where some of London's most famous shops are based, and which is almost always crammed with tourists. If you are keen on shopping—and have strong nerves and good shoes—by all means walk the full length of the street and back and end up festooned with bags. Oxford Street, reckoned to be the busiest shopping thoroughfare in Europe, runs west to east along the route of a Roman road from Marble Arch, via Oxford Circus to St. Giles Circus, where it intersects Charing Cross Road and Tottenham (pronounced, roughly: Tot-nmm) Court Road.

There are about 300 shops and department stores here, including the flagship stores for several major chains: Selfridges (founded in 1909, the second-largest department store in the UK after Harrods, and of interest to architecture buffs as well as consumers; it is noted for elaborate and imaginative window displays), Debenhams, John Lewis and Topshop, which boasts of being the largest fashion store in the world.

Architectural model of the Marble Arch, designed by John Nash c. 1826

Selfridges

Then & Now

Marble Arch

Carnaby Street, 1969

The Laughing Cavalier,
Franz Hals, 1624

3 At Oxford Circus, go to the south side of the street and take the first right turn after the entrance to the underground station, then walk straight on past the London Palladium theater: ahead of you is Liberty London, the famous department store which made Arts and Crafts designs popular and is usually an agreeable place to wander around. Liberty's distinctive patterned wares are of high quality and similar cost.

4 Near the east side of Liberty's is the entrance to the pedestrian zone of Carnaby Street—in the 1960s the main rival to the King's Road, Chelsea as the capital of "Swinging London." Approach with low expectations; there's nothing all that special here other than a famous photo op.

From here, retrace your steps to Oxford Circus and turn left on Oxford Street, take a right on Orchard Street and explore the much quieter streets of Marylebone, which can narrowly be defined as the northwest quadrant of the West End, though many people use it to mean pretty much the whole district included in today's walk; you can avoid confusion by thinking of this smaller area as Marylebone Village, bounded by Edgware Road to the wast, Marylebone Road to the north, Portland Place to the east and Oxford Street to the south.

5 One of the major higlights of this otherwise low-key area is a major art gallery. Turn right from Orchard Street onto Wigmore Street (the main west-east thoroughfare), then take a left and walk northwards into Manchester Square, where you will see Hertford House, the building which houses the Wallace Collection. This is, for its relatively modest size, an astonishingly rich collection. In London it is inevitably upstaged by the National Gallery and

Tate Britain (among others), but the 5,000 or so exhibits here are a feast. The Wallace is dedicated to both fine and decorative arts from the fifteenth to the nineteenth century, including porcelain, furniture, weaponry and the like. The paintings include works by Titian, Rembrandt, Rubens, Velazquez, Canaletto, Salvator Rosa, Joshua Reynolds and dozens of others; highlights include Franz Hals's *The Laughing Cavalier* and Nicolas Poussin's wonderful *Dance to the Music of Time* — a phrase that the novelist Anthony Powell used for his twelve-novel sequence about English life. The courtyard has recently been given a glass roof and serves as the restaurant Bagatelle.

6 Now return to Wigmore Street and find the Wigmore Hall, on the north side at No. 36. This is an intimate venue, but a distinguished one; since it opened in 1901, it has drawn performers of the highest rank: Enrico Caruso, Pablo Casals and Artur Rubinstein.

Pablo Casals

7 Wigmore Street is intersected by Wimpole Street, world-famous because of the play *The Barretts of Wimpole Street*, about the romance between the poets Elizabeth Barrett and Robert Browning. (Barrett lived at No. 50, though the building has since been redeveloped.) Wimpole Street is dense with literary associations: Alfred, Lord Tennyson mentions it in his long poem *In Memoriam*; the novelist Wilkie Collins lived here; and in Shaw's play *Pygmalion*, Prof. Henry Higgins lives at No. 272, which is where he teaches poor cockney Eliza Doolittle to talk proper.

Elizabeth Barrett

8 It is also the first of several places on this walk to play a part in the saga of the Beatles. No. 57 is a five-bed roomed house owned by the family of

Jane Asher, the young actress who in 1963 was Paul McCartney's girlfriend. Paul lodged on the top floor and wrote a number of the early Beatles songs here, including "I Want To Hold Your Hand" (John pounding away on a piano in the basement) and the music for "Yesterday," the most commercially successful song of all time. He moved a mile or so away to St. John's Wood in 1965.

9 From here make a left on New Cavendish Street and continue east to Portland Place; make a right. Ahead of you on the left-hand side of the street is All Souls Church, Langham Place. Immediately identifiable by its unique spire, it is the last place of worship designed by John Nash. It was completed at the end of 1823 and consecrated in 1824.

Langham Place c. 1900

10 Tired walkers often sit on the church's welcoming steps and watch politicians and celebrities walk by, because immediately to the north over the road is BBC Broadcasting House, home of BBC Radio. (BBC Television is based several miles west, in the White City district.) The building opened after about four years of construction in 1932, the same year that the BBC started transmitting some of the world's earliest television, using John Logie Baird's technology. The BBC (originally the British Broadcasting Company, now the Corporation) was founded in 1922 and began broadcasting from an address in the Strand; Broadcasting House, known to employees simply as "BH," was a purpose-made building, curved along its western side and intended to resemble an ocean liner, and also to echo Nash's church. Over its entrance stands a memorable statue by Eric Gill of Prospero and Ariel from Shakespeare's play *The Tempest*; it is said that when the Board of Governors first saw Gill's work, they were outraged by the size of Ariel's male member

and demanded that it be reduced. The inner entrance hall is very handsome in a modest way, but is not, strictly speaking, open to the uninvited. You could try pretending to be a visiting VIP.

11 Opposite All Souls Church to the west is the Langham Hotel, an upscale institution that opened in 1865 and was frequented by everyone from Napoleon III to Mark Twain. Here Oscar Wilde and Arthur Conan Doyle were commissioned to write *Picture of Dorian Gray* and *A Study in Scarlet*.

Arthur Conan Doyle

12 Keep walking northwards. If it is a weekday lunchtime and you have plenty of money with you, consider entering the R.I.B.A (Royal Institute of British Architects), walking up stairs and having a meal in one of the most exhilarating restaurants in London—high ceilings, high windows, splendid carvings (of stone as well as meat) and, in warm weather, a roof terrace.

13 When replete, continue north until you reach the southern edge of Regent's Park. Your next couple of hours, minimum, should be devoted to exploring and enjoying John Nash's admirable creation— both the park itself and its surroundings, including some very handsome terraces to the south, the east and some of the west. Nash worked on it from 1812–1826, and some consider it his masterpiece, an inspired balance of cultivated landscape, lake and architecture. In summer months, there are performances of Shakespeare's more crowd-pleasing plays in the Park's open-air theater.

14 To the north of the park is the London Zoo. If zoos trouble your conscience at all, either skip a visit (tickets are not cheap, because the zoo is largely self-supporting) or reflect on the fact that

since the 1980s this has developed into one of the most responsible zoos in the world, with appropriate environments for its thousands of inmates, and a far-sighted breeding program. It is also—more by chance than design—a compendium of strange and interesting buildings, from the delightful Penguin Pool of the 1930s to the 1960s Aviary, designed by Lord Snowdon. Fans of the cult English film *Withnail and I* should make a pilgrimage to the point outside the wolf enclosure where the anti-hero delivers a soliloquy from *Hamlet*.

15 Before leaving this area, take a short walk just to the north and visit Primrose Hill, where you can have a panoramic view of pretty much all Central London, except the parts that have been blocked by ugly buildings from the fifties and sixties.

16 The next part of the walk is an optional extra: a digression into the largely residential district of St. John's Wood, where there are two English institutions of note: Lord's Cricket Ground, sacred to the great game, and Abbey Road Studios, sacred to music of all kinds, and particularly to the memory of a certain beat combo from Liverpool. To reach Lord's, leave the park at one of its northwest exits and turn right onto Prince Albert Road, then cross the roundabout and keep going in the same south-westerly direction along St. John's Wood Road.

Lord's, which with some justice calls itself "the home of cricket," opened for play in 1814; there had been two previous incarnations on nearby sites—from 1787 to 1810, and then for a couple of years from 1811 to 1813—when it was demolished to make way for the Regent's Canal development. The best-known part of Lord's is its late-Victorian Pavilion (built 1889-90), which houses the famous

Long Room—through which teams have to walk on their way to the playing field—changing rooms, a handsome bar and other amenities. Lord's also contains the world's earliest museum devoted to a sport. The ground is owned by the Marylebone Cricket Club, or MCC.

🛈 To reach Abbey Road Studios, carry on down St. John's Wood Road and turn right onto Grove End Road, which after a slight curve to the right becomes Abbey Road. Abbey Road Studios is at No. 3. The building was originally a private residence and was bought by the Gramophone Co. (later EMI), which converted it into studios and specialized in classical music, notably the famous Beethoven recordings by Artur Schnabel. In the late fifties it became a factory for pop music; on June 6, 1962 the Beatles cut their first single, "Love Me Do", here. Over the years, its increasingly complex facilities have been used by many British acts, from Pink Floyd to Radiohead. The iconic cover shot of the *Abbey Road* album was taken on August 8, 1969, by Iain MacMillan. Countless thousands of fans have re-staged it ever since.

Then & Now

Abbey Road

18 End of digression. If you have skipped St. John's Wood, simply complete your tour around Regent's Park; if not, return to the park then leave at its southwest exit, cross over onto Park Road and take an almost immediate left onto Baker Street. In the Baker Street area, you will find— what else?—The Sherlock Holmes Museum, which is legally allowed to use the address "221b Baker Street" by the authority of the City of London, though its neighbors are Nos. 237 and 241, so a pedant would insist that it actually occupies No. 239.

For many years, the Museum disputed its right to the 221b address with the Abbey National Building Society, whose premises stood where Holmes's flat would have been situated had it existed; in a charming act of whimsy unusual in a major financial institution, the Abbey used to employ a secretary to answer the hundreds of letters for the Great Detective that arrived there every year. The dispute ended in 2002 when the Abbey moved out.

19 Just a few doors away at No. 231 is a shop dedicated to the Beatles. It is said to be well-stocked and pricey, but with friendly staff; a good place, maybe, for fans to pick up souvenirs while the memory of Abbey Road is still fresh.

20 You do not need to be a great detective yourself to notice the marks of Sherlock all over the Baker Street area, from the rather attractive murals in Baker Street Station to the statue of Holmes at the Marylebone Road entrance, erected in 1999.

21 To the east of Baker Street station are the veteran tourist attractions, Madame Tussaud's and the London Planetarium. To each his own.

22 Head west to Marylebone Station, filmed for the opening sequence of *A Hard Day's Night*.

23 This whole area of London is something of a happy hunting ground for Beatles loyalists. One hotspot can be found by returning to Marylebone Road and turning onto Upper Montagu Street. Ringo Starr used to lease a two-floor apartment just a couple of blocks south of here at No. 34 Montagu Square, which became the center for all kinds of wild activities. Ringo soon moved out, and Paul McCartney took over for a while, converting part of the space into a recording studio. He wrote "Eleanor Rigby" while living here and made some recordings for the Apple subsidiary Zapple Records; the avant-garde American novelist William S. Burroughs came here to put some readings on tape for Zapple. Jimi Hendrix then lived at No. 34 for a while, with a bandmate and their two girlfriends; his Montagu Square composition was "The Wind Cries Mary." Finally, John Lennon and Yoko Ono took up occupancy during the recording of the Beatles' "White Album" and their own collaboration *Two Virgins*, reducing the place to squalor. The cover of *Two Virgins* is a naked shot of John and Yoko, taken in the apartment. John and Yoko were busted by the police on suspicion of possessing drugs, but Yoko seems not to have held a grudge; in 2010, she unveiled a commemorative plaque on No. 34.

Marylebone Station in
A Hard Day's Night, 1964

Close your circle by wandering all the way down Montagu Street, turning right onto Seymour Street and then right onto Great Cumberland Place, returning to Marble Arch—where you can either end the walk and hop on the Central Line, or enjoy the open spaces of Hyde Park and its main lake, the Serpentine.

Jimmy Hendrix poses in
Montague Square

THE CITY

N

London

City Rd

Old Street

Kings Square
Garden

Goswell Rd

Old St

Spa Fields
Park

Farringdon Rd

Theobald's Rd

Grays Inn Rd

Clearkenwell

Bunhill
Fields

Barbican

City of London
Girls School

City Rd

Farringdon St

Barbican

Aldergate St

Moorgate

Bishopsgate

London
Smithfield Market

London Wall

Liverpool St

Chauncery Lane

High Holborn

Newgate St

Postman's
Park

Moorgate

Holborn

Fetter Ln

City

St. Paul's

Cheapside

Prince's St

Threadneedle St

Houndsditch

Bevis Marks

2

5 6 3

Fleet St

4

7

8

1

St. Paul's Church Yard

17

Bank

16 15

9

New Bridge St

City
Thameslink

Queen St Pl

18

Cornhill

Leadenhall St

14

Aldgate

Temple
Gardens

Blackfriars

19

20

12 13

Fenchurch St

Victoria Embankment

Queen Victoria St

Mansion House

Cannon St

Gracechurch St

Temple

10

Upper Thames St

Cannon St

Monument

King William St

Lower Thames St

Monument

Tower Hill

Tower Hill

River Thames

Blackfriars
Bridge

Millennium
Bridge

Southwark
Bridge

London
Bridge

Tower of
London

Bernie Spain
Gardens

Southwark

London Bridge

Tooley St

London Bridge

Tower
Bridge

Stamford St

Blackfriars Rd

Southwark St

St. Thomas St

Potters
Fields Park

Waterloo E

Southwark

Borough High St

Guy's
Hospital

Crucifix Ln

Waterloo

The Cut

Marshalsea Rd

Leathermarket
Gardens

Waterloo
Station

Baylis Rd

Waterloo Rd

Borough

Long Ln

A302

Lambeth N

The Borough

Tower Bridge Rd

Westminster Br Rd

St. Garden Row

Borough Rd

A3

Great Dover St

Abbey St

Kennington Rd

Lambeth Rd

London Rd

Geraldine
Mary
Ausworth Park

St. George's Rd

Elephant & Castle

Tower Bridge Rd

Grange Rd

1000 ft

Elephant & Castle

New Kent Rd

Old Kent Rd

200 m

Heygate St

START:
St. Paul's Cathedral

TUBE:
St. Paul's

END:
St. Mary Woolnoth

TUBE:
Monument

London, St. Paul's Cathedral, by Camille Pissarro, 1890

Christopher Wren

St. Paul's Cathedral viewed from Millennium Bridge

The City of London—known simply as "the City"—is London's equivalent of Wall Street. It is also known as the Square Mile, since that is roughly its area. Settled 2,000 years ago, it was once completely enclosed by walls, and the frequent suffix "-gate" indicates the ancient entrances to the City. It was this area that was burned so badly in the Great Fire of 1666, and the Monument to the Fire, co-designed by Christopher Wren, is one of the City's most conspicuous landmarks, as is Wren's masterpiece, St. Paul's Cathedral, a post-Fire replacement for the severely damaged older church.

Begin from the St. Paul's Undergound station on the Central Line.

1 Arrive at St. Paul's Cathedral, preferably after walking across the river to it on the new-ish and

already well-loved Millennium Bridge. The fifth
cathedral to stand on this site, it is a glorious
thing, probably the greatest building in London.
It is a national disgrace that post-1945 developers
were allowed to surround this jewel with dull,
tawdry modern buildings. St. Paul's was an almost
miraculous survivor of Nazi bombing. It took
several direct hits, including one by an incendiary
bomb that would have blown it to pieces had a brave
soldier not defused it. This happy fluke of bombing
patterns made the Cathedral a potent emblem of
London's wartime endurance; of humanity resisting
barbarism. In the words of the visionary architecture
critic Ian Nairn, writing in the 1960s: "It is a
stupendous, encompassing achievement of balanced
feeling and maturity... It is hard not to sound like a

Then & Now

Left: Fleet Street, 1924; Right: *Fleet Street*, by James Valentine c. 1890.

Left: Fleet Street c. 1850s; Right: Present

Zeppelin flies over St. Paul's Cathedral, 1930

New *Daily Telegraph* Offices Fleet Street, 1882

bad Churchillian parody, but in fact this is why we fought the war."

The Churchillian note is appropriate: When St. Paul's was hit in the Blitz it was he who re-directed all of the local fire-fighting units to save it from flames, and Churchill—like the former masters of war, Nelson and Wellington—had his funeral here. Today, the Cathedral evokes all manner of other, less patriotic responses. Most people find it an uplifting place. Some large buildings are totalitarian monsters, designed to cow and to crush the powerless onlooker; St. Paul's manages to feel intimate as well as grand—an invitation upwards, beyond human pettiness and into infinity. It is worth recalling that Newton's *Principia Mathematica* (1687) is a product of the same culture that generated the Cathedral, which was begun in 1669 and finally declared complete (though it wasn't quite) in 1711. Wren's work speaks of the beginnings of modern science, of the optimism of a nation that had somehow survived the horrors of civil war, and of a brief period when the inevitable conflicts between religion and science had not yet grown bitter.

2 After seeing the sublime, it is time for a venture into the grubbier aspects of the City's past. Go due west along Ludgate Hill, take a quick diversion to the right on Ludgate Hill and go up the Old Bailey—otherwise known as the Central Criminal Court—on the street of the same name. The current courthouse dates to 1902.

3 Then come back and continue Ludgate Hill until it becomes Fleet Street. Fleet Street, which until the 1980s was the home to most of Britain's national newspapers, became a synonym for the press—a synonym still used from time to time, though those papers now issue from Wapping, Docklands and elsewhere. *The Times*, launched in 1785, was near here in Printing House Square until 1974, when it moved to Gray's Inn Road; the *Observer*, launched in 1711, was a neighbor from 1969–88; the *Daily Mail* was on Carmelite Street from 1897 to 1927, then Tudor Street from 1927–89; the *Daily Mirror* in Whitefriar's Street (1905–20) and then at Fetter Lane (1920–61); the *Daily Express* in Shoe Lane (1900–33); the *Daily Telegraph* on Fleet Street itself (1862–1987); the *News of the World* on Bouverie Street (1892–1986), and, also on Bouverie Street, the *Sun* (1969–86).

4 The appearance of St. Bride's Church—off to your left—has been vastly influential, in a most unusual way. Its immediately recognizable spire, which was added to the church by Wren, inspired a local baker to create the first tiered wedding cake, so establishing a custom still honored at traditional weddings to this day. The church stands on the grounds of a much earlier place of worship, devoted to a Celtic deity some 2,000 years ago. It was consecrated as a Christian church in the sixth century, sacred to St. Bridget, and then rebuilt a few times, most extensively in the fifteenth century.

5 Next up on your right is the passage that leads to Dr. Samuel Johnson's House in Gough Square. An unfashionable writer these days, partly because of his robust Tory politics and Anglican faith, but mainly because eighteenth century prose is unpalatable to those who only read modern books, Samuel Johnson is nonetheless a giant of English literature. As Shakespeare to our drama, and Dickens to our fiction, so Johnson to our discursive prose. A profoundly troubled soul—Johnson suffered from what we would now call depression— he somehow managed to complete a number of

Dr. Samuel Johnson

James Boswell

projects that might easily have taken an ordinary mortal an entire lifetime. His accomplishments include a set of biographies devoted to the English poets (it has been said that the only reason Johnson is not considered the father of modern biography is that the title belongs to his younger friend James Boswell, for his *Life of Johnson*); a critical commentary on Shakespeare; a light but profound short fiction, *Rasselas*; essays of all kinds; some of the best English poems of the eighteenth century, above all "The Vanity of Human Wishes"; and his most famous achievement, his *Dictionary*, not by any means the first of its kind, but a staggering feat that has set the pattern for all subsequent English dictionaries. Johnson started his great labor in 1746, and lived in this house from 1748 to 1758, writing on his own in the attic, while, in the rooms below, a team of clerks did the work of chasing references and compiling his entries. He had expected the task to take three years; it took nine years, and was finally completed in 1755, when the first edition was published to immense acclaim from around the world. It was unrivalled for a century and a half, and is a fine book for browsing, full of pungent phrasing and unexpected quirks. The museum charges a modest fee; worth it.

6 Next, treat yourself to a drink or a snack just a few yards away in the Cheshire Cheese, or, as most guide books call it, Ye Olde Cheshire Cheese, where Johnson almost certainly ate and drank. A plaque identifies his favorite seat. Though crowded, it is still a good pub, with plenty of character.

7 Fleet Street was also, of course, the home of Sweeney Todd, the Demon Barber. If he existed—not everyone is convinced—he is said to have plied his deadly trade at No. 186, which has been demolished. He is said to have killed some 150 victims, which would make him by far the worst serial killer in British history. The Sondheim musical is true to the main outlines of the story: Todd had built a special chair, which would pitch backwards and dispatch freshly dead bodies down into a cellar; Todd's lover, Margery Lovett, brought them by tunnel to the basement of her pie shop in Bell Yard, where she chopped them up and made them into pies. Believe it if you wish.

8 Carry on a little further and cross the road to visit Prince Henry's Room at No. 17, originally a pub, later many other things including a waxworks, and today a small museum dedicated to the diarist Samuel Pepys.

9 Next, you should wander toward the river and into the two Inns of Court. All barristers in England and Wales must belong to one of four such professional societies. With their manicured lawns and historic buildings, the Inner Temple and Middle Temple make for an atmospheric and imposing sight. This land used to belong to the Knights Templar, hence the Temple name.

10 Now enjoy a breath of Thames air on the Victoria Embankment, walk eastwards and turn left onto Blackfriar's, the name of which recalls a Dominican monastery which stood here from the thirteenth century until the Reformation. Then go right, onto Queen Victoria Street, until you reach Mansion House Underground station.

11 Take the road that forks to the right, Cannon Street, and keep going until you reach the Monument. Co-designed by Christopher Wren and the astonishingly gifted scientist Robert Hooke in

Inner Temple

Middle Temple

Victoria Embankment, by Lesser Ury, 1926

1671–77, it alludes to a Roman original, and has a coded reference to the Fire itself: the 205 feet of its height symbolizes its distance from the shop on Pudding Lane where the Fire started.

12 Then head north up Gracechurch Street, which is the path to Leadenhall Market and the Lloyd's Building. Leadenhall Market, which dates from 1881, is now an agreeable place to have lunch or a drink in one of many bars and cafés, while enjoying the surviving late-Victorian surroundings.

Leadenhall Market, 1881

13 The Lloyd's building is a striking example of modern architecture that appeals to all but the most dogged traditionalists. A collaborative effort by the architect Richard Rogers and the engineering company of Ove Arup, constructed from 1978–1986, it defies convention by locating all its major service functions on the outside. Not everyone admires it, but those who do so think it one of the best sights in town, especially when lit up at night.

14 Carry on a short distance to the east to see St. Katherine Cree church, which predates the Fire (it was built 1628–31): Purcell and Handel both used the organ here.

15 Proceed up Creechurch Lane and left into Bevis Marks for the Spanish and Portuguese Synagogue. The oldest building of its kind in England, the Synagogue was made in 1701 by a Quaker architect, Joseph Avis, who at the end of his task handed his fee back to the congregation: a moving gesture of respect between religious faiths. A London synagogue had become essential after the flood of Jewish immigration to the City that followed Cromwell's resettlement legislation, encouraging expelled Jews to return to England, in 1655. One of the main beams was donated by Queen Anne, to confirm that monarchs as well as republicans were now glad to welcome Jewish immigrants.

16 To the left is the Swiss Re Tower (completed in 2004), a curvy, glass-surfaced building more commonly known as the Gherkin. The Swiss Re Tower, like many other examples of good (and surprisingly popular) modern buildings in London, is the work of Sir Norman Foster.

17 Bevis Marks leads into Camomile Street; turn left here and head left onto Bishopsgate, then take the right fork which is Threadneedle Street, and ahead of you is the Bank of England, which has its own museum. The Bank was originally founded to raise money for a war against France, in 1694; today its principal jobs include managing the national debt and issuing banknotes.

18 To the south of the Bank is Mansion House, built on the site of the old Stock Exchange in 1752. This is the official home of the Lord Mayor of London, notional head of the City (not to be confused with the Mayor of London, who is the mayor of the entire city of Greater London).

Mansion House, by J. Woods after a picture by Hablot Browne & R. Garland, published 1837

19 Just a few steps away is St. Stephen Walbrook Church, designed by Wren from 1672–80, on the site once occupied by an ancient Roman temple.

20 Nearby, on Lombard Street is St. Mary Woolnoth (1714–1730), designed by Nicholas Hawksmoor, and one of his masterpieces.

From here it is a quick walk down King William Street to the Monument station on the Circle and District lines.

SOUTH BANK

1 St. Thomas' Hospital
2 Old County Hall
3 London Eye
4 Jubilee Gardens
5 Royal Festival Hall
6 BFI Southbank
7 Royal National Theatre
8 Oxo Building
9 Founders Arms
10 Tate Modern
11 Millennium Bridge
12 Cardinal's Wharf

13 The Globe
14 The Clink Prison Museum
15 The Golden Hind
16 Southwark Cathedral
17 Borough Market
18 Old Operating Theatre Museum
   and Herb Garret
19 H.M.S. Belfast
20 Design Museum
21 Tower Bridge
22 Tower of London

N

London

TOUR NINE SOUTH BANK

Laman St

Aldgate High St

Mansell St

E. Smithfield

Shad Thames

Jamaica Rd

Aldgate East

Aldgate

Tower Hill

Tower Hill

22

21

Tower Bridge

20

Fenchurch St

Lower Thames St

The Queen's Walk

Tower Bridge Rd

Potters Fields Park

City Hall

19

Tooley St

St. Thomas St

Crucifix Ln

Leathermarket Gardens

Gracechurch St

Monument

King William St

London Bridge

London Bridge

18

Guy's Hospital

Long Ln

Great Dover St

Bank

Prince's St

London Bridge

16

London Bridge

Cannon St

Cannon St

15

17

14

Borough High St

Borough

New Kent Rd

Mansion House

Upper Thames St

Southwark Bridge

13

Marshalsea Rd

ul's

St. Paul's Church Yard

Queen Victoria St

11

12

10

Southwark St

Southwark

Union St

Borough Rd

Elephant & Castle

St. Paul's Cathedral

9

Blackfriars

The Borough

City Thameslink

New Bridge St

Blackfriars Rd - Southwark

Blackfriars Bridge

The Cut

Fleet St

8

Waterloo E

Waterloo Rd

Westminster Br Rd

St. George's Rd

Geraldine Mary Harmsworth Park

Bernie Spain Gardens

Stamford St

Baylis Rd

Kennington Rd

Waterloo

Lambeth N

Lambeth Rd

Temple

Victoria Embankment

7

Waterloo Rd

Waterloo

York Rd

Lambeth Palace Rd

Archbishop's Park

Kingsway

Aldwych

Strand

6

5

Waterloo Bridge

Jubilee Gardens

4

2

1

Westminster Bridge

3

River Thames

Embankment

Lambeth Bridge

1000 ft

200 m

Covent Garden

Charing Cross

Westminster

Bridge St

Abingdon St

START:
St. Thomas' Hospital

TUBE:
━━ ━━ Waterloo Station
━━ ━━

END:
The Tower of London

TUBE:
━━ ━━ Tower Hill

Florence Nightingale

The Globe Theatre

This is very simple and, in fine weather, mostly cheerful and uplifting walk which essentially hugs the southern bank of the Thames before crossing over to the Tower. It takes in the large-scale artistic complex of the South Bank and then the attractions, both old and modern, of the fascinating district of Southwark. Remember to keep looking left at the river as well as right at the landmarks—some of the best vistas of the city are to be had from this vantage point. Breezes from the Thames tend to keep it cool on all but the most sultry of days.

Start at Waterloo Station and walk south and slightly west down York Road, following the curve for a few yards until it joins Westminster Bridge Road, the A302. The Bridge is directly ahead.

1 Just south of Westminster Bridge is St. Thomas' Hospital, a large and distinguished institution, which has been here since the ancient foundation moved from its original home near London Bridge in the Victorian period. The Hospital is home to the Florence Nightingale Museum.

2 On the other side of Westminster Bridge is the Old County Hall, former headquarters of the London County Council and then, until its abolition in 1986, of the Greater London Council (an organization alternately celebrated and damned as an ultra-left-wing body in the 1970s and '80s). It is now home to the London Aquarium and a permanent exhibition of works by Surrealist Salvador Dalí.

3 This whole district is now dominated by perhaps the best-loved of the city's recent landmarks, the London Eye, with its 32 capsules. Originally intended as a temporary structure, it now seems set for a very long run. The wheel revolves a complete circle every 45 minutes.

4 After the Jubilee Gardens, created in 1977 for the Queen's Silver Jubilee, is the South Bank, London's most concentrated gathering of leading artistic institutions: by turn, the Royal Festival Hall, the Hayward Gallery, the Queen Elizabeth Hall & Purcell Room, the BFI Southbank (still known to most people as the National Film Theatre) and the National Theatre, today known as the Royal National Theatre. These have all sprung up, on what was mostly waste land, since 1951, year of

Then & Now

St. Thomas' Hospital

the Festival of Britain, an event designed both to commemorate the Great Exhibition of 1851 and to cheer up an impoverished, war-exhausted nation in the years of austerity following the end of WWII.

5 Royal Festival Hall—oldest of the South Bank buildings and to many people's eyes far and away the most attractive (it was designed by Robert Matthew)—is for concerts, both classical and popular. There is a first-rate, and not terrifyingly expensive restaurant on the upper floor, which used to be known as the "People's Palace" but has now been re-branded as the Skylon. The view of the river is one of the best to be had anywhere in London. The Hayward Gallery, unappealing to the eye from the outside, plays host to large-scale visiting exhibitions, usually of modern artists or artistic movements.

6 The BFI Southbank/National Film Theatre is probably the best arts cinema in Britain, and specializes in intelligently programmed seasons devoted to directors, stars, national film industries, production units and the like. The space between the BFI and the river is often the site of a second-hand book market, where the prices are reasonable. The BFI also runs an IMAX cinema; turn right and walk southwards for about 150 yards.

7 The National Theatre, now officially called the Royal National Theatre (though almost no one uses the full name in everyday speech) was finally completed in 1976 and drew a great deal of criticism at the time for its willfully ugly, bunker-like appearance, more suitable for a prison or nuclear power station than a palace of the dramatic arts. No one could think it lovely, but Londoners have grown used to it with the years, and have learned to pay more attention to the qualities of the plays produced than the brutality of its design. It specializes in ambitious productions of classic plays, both English-language and from around the world, and in new writing by established playwrights and rising talents. There are three main spaces—the Olivier, the Cottesloe and the Littleton—and also an informal concert area on the ground floor where musicians give free shows.

8 After the South Bank, quicken your pace a little, perhaps pausing for a quick visit to the Oxo Tower, or to have lunch in its well-reviewed restaurant. The building has long been well known for a witty evasion of regulations about commercial display. Told that they could not advertise their brand with billboards, the Oxo company re-designed the windows so that they spelled out OXO.

9 If thirsty, stop for a pint at the Founders Arms, 52 Hopton St., which is built on the site where the bells for St. Paul's were cast.

10 Now proceed as directly as you can to Tate Modern. The museum is unmissable—a huge former power station, designed by Giles Gilbert Scott (1947) and converted as one of the Millennium projects. The vast atrium of Tate Modern—which has free admission and is pretty breathtaking on first sight—is used to display commissioned works from leading artists around the world. As its name suggests, this branch of the Tate is dedicated to all things modern, including photographic, video and conceptual works as well as paintings and sculptures. It combines permanent collections with large-scale shows. The bookshop is large and thoroughly stocked; browsing recommended for all modern art fans.

11 If the weather is fine, you should definitely take a stroll on the Millennium Bridge, which has overcome its growing pains—it wobbled—and is now the most agreeable way to cross from south to north banks.

12 Keep heading east and have a quick look at Cardinal's Wharf, an unusually well-preserved terrace from the seventeenth century. Rumor has it that Christopher Wren had quarters here at No. 49 while working on St Paul's.

No. 49, white building (left)

13 Next comes Shakespeare's Globe—a fairly accurate recreation of the theater that Shakespeare's company constructed in 1599, and which stood very close to here on land which has since been developed into buildings. In summer months—productions are staged between late April and October—you can watch Shakespeare's plays in pretty much the same way that the Elizabethans would have seen them, in the open air. The Globe also stages other works from the Elizabethan and Jacobean periods, and some modern plays with suitable subject matter, such as Howard Brenton's *Anne Boleyn*.

Then & Now

Shakespeare's Globe

The International Shakespeare Globe Centre

14 Before the play, you might want to remind yourself of just how depraved Southwark used to be by visiting The Clink Prison Museum, which is built on the site of The Clink, a foul and notorious lock-up from 1151 to 1780.

15 Close by the Clink, dry-docked in St. Mary Overy's Wharf is a replica of the *Golden Hind* (or *Hinde*), the ship in which Sir Francis Drake circumnavigated the globe between 1577–1580.

16 Southwark Cathedral, though it has only enjoyed Cathedral status since 1905, has been a place of worship for a thousand years. The main structure, which has been unsentimentally described as "a large friendly lump of a building" is medieval— circa 1220 to 1420; the nave is a Victorian reconstruction. Geoffrey Chaucer knew it; William Shakespeare would have known it, and possibly used it as his chosen place of worship—there is an odd, and some think sinister, carving of him in the south nave aisle; the poet's brother Edmund Shakespeare was buried here in 1607. The great Anglican theologian and writer Lancelot Andrewes is buried near the High Altar.

Then & Now

Borough Market, c. 1860

17 Turn right where London Bridge touches the bank and walk south towards Borough High Street and Borough Market. It was established in 1756 and is London's oldest fruit and vegetable market to be held on the same site.

18 Then, for another out-of-the-ordinary experience, highly recommended to those of a scientific or morbid disposition, head east down St. Thomas Street to visit, at No 9a, the Old Operating Theatre Museum and Herb Garret, a remnant of the old St. Thomas' Hospital before it moved west to its present home in Lambeth.

19 Carry on along the riverbank until you reach the place where *H.M.S. Belfast* is docked. This former Royal Naval vessel, which helped sink the German cruiser *Scharnhorst* in 1943, has been a museum since 1971; small boys love it.

20 If you're interested in design, walk a little further east past the curvy City Hall (designed by Norman Foster as an ecologically friendly home for the London Assembly) and visit the white-fronted Design Museum, the such museum in the world.

21 Otherwise, cross Tower Bridge (built 1886–1894) which rivals Westminster Palace as a universally recognized symbol of London.

22 On the opposite bank of the Thames is the Tower of London, the earliest parts of which were built almost a thousand years ago by William the Conqueror as a citadel for keeping rebellious Anglo-Saxons quiet. One of the oldest extant parts is the White Tower, built in 1078, though this structure has been substantially restored in a more yellowish stone that some find unsympathetic.

The Tower has undergone several stages of development and extension since William's day, particularly under Richard I, who developed the Inner Ward, and then under Edward I, who was responsible for the Outer Ward. A fairly large part of the castle has remained substantially unchanged since 1285, though the mock-medieval exterior wall was put up in the 1840s. (You need to keep your eyes sharp on this tour, as the architectural fakery and pastiche stands cheek by jowl with the genuine.) Two parts of the Tower that deserve your closest attention are the Tudor chapel of St. Peter ad Vincula and the Chapel of St. John on the first floor of the White Tower.

The Tower has a fairly grim reputation, not all of it deserved, since it has served many worthy functions over the years—as the treasury, as the Royal Mint, and from 1669 onwards, as the repository of the Crown Jewels, some of which used to be housed in the Palace of Westminster's Jewel Tower. The Jewels are more than just gaudy sparklers; many of them were made for Charles II and are quite fine. Reports of Anne Boleyn's headless ghost, and other strange spirits, still crop up from time to time.

Anne Boleyn

Two Princes Edward and Richard in the Tower, 1483, by Sir John Everett Millais, 1878

Almost every schoolchild used to know the tale of the "Princes in the Tower," the two young heirs to the throne, Edward and Richard, who were supposedly murdered by Richard III in 1483. Elizabeth I was imprisoned here for a while by Mary, and the Tower continued to be the place where dangerous prisoners were held as late as 1941, when the mysterious Nazi leader Rudolf Hess was incarcerated after his flight from Germany. The last person to be executed here, by firing squad, was the Nazi spy Joseph Jacobs, also in 1941. Curious fact: Only a handful of prisoners were actually put to death within the precincts of the Tower itself; the main execution site was outside the wall, on Tower Hill. Today, the Tower is a UNESCO World Heritage Site.

The nearest Underground station is Tower Hill on the Circle and District lines.

Executions in the Tower of London

The following seven nobles are known to have been executed on the Tower Green:

Margaret Pole

Catherine Howard

Lady Jane Grey

Robert Devereux

1. **William Hastings**, 1st Baron Hastings, by order of the Richard, Duke of Gloucester, in 1483.
2. **Queen Anne Boleyn**, second wife of King Henry VIII, 19 May, 1536.
3. **Margaret Pole**, Countess of Salisbury, the last of the Plantagenet dynasty on 27 May 1541.
4. **Queen Catherine Howard**, fifth wife of Henry VIII, by a Bill of attainder on 13 February 1542.
5. **Jane Boleyn**, Viscountess Rochford, by order of Henry VIII on 13 February 1542.
6. **Lady Jane Grey**, the Nine Days Queen, wife of Lord Guilford Dudley, by order of a special commission for High Treason, on 12 February 1554.
7. **Robert Devereux**, 2nd Earl of Essex for treason on 25 February 1601.

The Tower of London Map

1 The White Tower

The oldest part of the complex, built by William the Conqueror. The name "White Tower" probably refers when it was painted white during the reign of Henry III. Located on the second floor, the Chapel of St. John the Evangelist is where Mary I was betrothed to Philip of Spain by proxy (he wasn't present) here in 1554.

2 Chapel Royal of St. Peter ad Vincula

The parish church of the Tower and burial place of many executed here. (The Chapel in the White Tower was only for the sovereign and the court.)

3 Tower Green and Scaffold Site

Seven famous prisoners were executed here. The private executions took place on the Tower Green within the walls of the Tower to avoid embarrassing the prisoner or the monarch. Normally, the executions took place outside on Tower Hill and were usually viewed by thousands of spectators.

4 The Queen's House

Originally, the Lieutenant of the Tower lived here and was the custodian of several famous prisoners: Guy Fawkes, Lady Jane Grey and Anne Boleyn.

5 The Bell Tower

Several famous prisoners were held in the Bell Tower during Tudor times, including Sir Thomas More and the Princess Elizabeth.

6 Traitor's Gate

Many famous prisoners arrived at the Tower here, including the Princess Elizabeth, when she was imprisoned by her sister Mary.

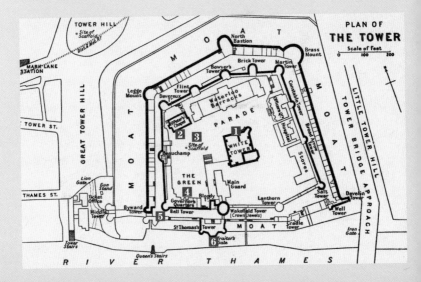

PLAN OF
THE TOWER

INDEX

RECOMMENDED READING

Anyone who wishes to pursue matters touched on in this book might care to consult some of its major sources.

Ackroyd, Peter, *London: The Biography* (London, Chatto & Windus, 2000)

Ashley, Morris, *England in the Seventeenth Century* (Harmondsworth; Penguin, 1952)

Belloc, Hilaire, *Charles I, King of England* (London, Cassell, 1933)

Benson, E.F., *Sir Francis Drake* (London, Bodley Head, 1932)

Bindoff, S.T., *Tudor England* (Harmondsworth, Penguin, revised edition 1978)

Bostridge, Mark, *Florence Nightingale: the Woman and her Legend* (London, Viking, 2008)

Brigden, Susan, *Reformation London* (Oxford: Clarendon, 1991)

Brigden, Susan *New Worlds, Lost Worlds: The Rule of the Tudors 1485-1603* (London, Penguin, 2000)

Brown, R. Allen, *The Normans and the Norman Conquest* (London, Boydell; revised edition 2000)

Burgess, Anthony, *Shakespeare* (Harmondsworth, Penguin, 1970)

Burgess, Anthony, *A Dead Man in Deptford* (London, Hutchinson, 1993)

Calder, Angus, *The People's War: Britain 1939-1945* (London, Pimlico, 1992)

Churchill, Winston: *A History of the English-Speaking Peoples:*
Volume I: The Birth of Britain (London, Cassell, 1956)
Volume II: The New World (London, Cassell, 1956)
Volume II: The Age of Revolution (London, Cassell, 1957)
Volume IV: The Great Democracies (London, Cassell, 1958)

Deighton, Len, *Len Deighton's London Dossier* (Harmondsworth, Penguin, 1967)

Dillon, Brian, *Tormented Hope: Nine Hypochondriac Lives* (London, Penguin, 2009)

Bindoff, St.T., *Tudor England* (Harmondsworth, Penguin, 1981)

Dudley Edwards, Owen, *The Quest for Sherlock Holmes* (Edinburgh, Mainstream, 1983)

Ellmann, Richard, *Oscar Wilde* (London, Hamish Hamilton, 1987)

Inwood, Stephen, *A History of London* (London, Macmillan, 1998)

Fletcher, Geoffrey, *The London Nobody Knows* (Harmondsworth, Penguin, 1965)

Fraser, Antonia, *Mary, Queen of Scots* (London, Phoenix, revised edition 2009)

Fraser, Antonia (ed.), *The Lives of the Kings and Queens of England* (London, Phoenix, revised edition 1999)

Frayling, Christopher, *Nightmare: the Birth of Horror* (London, BBC, 1996)

Gill, Stephen, *William Wordsworth: A Life* (Oxford, OUP, 1990)

Glinert, Ed, *The London Compendium* (London, Allen Lane, 2003)

Hibbert, Christopher, *Queen Victoria, a Personal History* (London, HarperCollins, 2001)

Hibbert, Christopher, *Charles I* (London, Macmillan, revised edition 2007)

Hibbert, Christopher, *The London Encyclopaedia, 3rd Edition* (London, Macmillan, 2010)

Hill, Christopher, *God's Englishman: Oliver Cromwell and the English Revolution* (London, Penguin, revised edition 1990)

Hill, Christopher, *Reformation to Industrial Revolution* (London, Weidenfeld & Nicolson, 1967)

Hobsbawm, Eric, *The Age of Revolution, 1789-1848* (London, Weidenfeld & Nicolson, 1962)

Hobsbawm, Eric, *The Age of Capital, 1848-1875* (London, Weidenfeld & Nicolson, 1975)

Hobsbawm, Eric, *The Age of Empire, 1875-1914* (London, Weidenfeld & Nicolson, 1985)

Holmes, George, *The Later Middle Ages, 1272-1485* (London, Thomas Nelson, 1962)

Hopkins, R. Thurston, *This London: Its Taverns, Haunts and Memories* (London, Cecil Palmer, 1927)

Jackson, Holbrook, *The 1890s* (London, Hutchinson, 1968)

Jackson, Kevin: *Fast: Feasting on the Streets of London* (London, Portobello Books, 2006)

Jackson, Kevin, *The Worlds of John Ruskin* (London, Pallas Athene, 2009)

Jenkins, Roy, *Churchill* (London, Macmillan, 2001)

Johnson, Edgar, *Charles Dickens, His Tragedy and Triumph* (Revised edition: Harmondsworth, Penguin, 1977)

Jusserand, J.J., *English Wayfaring Life in the Middle Ages* (London, Methuen, 1951)

MacDonald, Ian, *Revolution in the Head: The Beatles' Records in the Sixties* (London, 4th Estate, 1994)

Macaulay, Lord, *The History of England* (Abridged edition: London, Penguin Classics, 1986)

Mayhew, *London Labour and the London Poor* (London; Cosimo re-issue, 2009)

Mitchell, R.J and Leys, M.D.R., *A History of London Life* (Harmondsworth, Penguin, 1968)

Moore, Alan, *From Hell* (London, Knockabout, 2008)

Motion, Andrew, *John Keats* (London, Faber, 1997)

Myers, A.R., *England in the Late Middle Ages* (Harmondsworth, Penguin, 1952, revised 1966)

Nairn, Ian, *Nairn's London* (Harmondsworth, Penguin, 1966)

Nicholl, Charles, *The Reckoning: The Murder of Christopher Marlowe* (London, Cape, 1992)

Nicholl, Charles, *The Lodger: Shakespeare on Silver Street* (London, Allen Lane, 2007)

Picard, Liza, *Restoration London* (London, Weidenfeld & Nicolson, 1997)

Picard, Liza, *Dr. Johnson's London* (London, Weidenfeld & Nicolson, 2000)

Plumb, J.H., *England in the Eighteenth Century* (Harmondsworth, Penguin, 1950, 1973)

Pope-Hennessy, Una, *Charles Dickens* (Harmondsworth, Penguin, 1970)

Porter, Roy, *London: A Social History* (London, Hamish Hamilton, 1994)

Richardson, John, *The Annals of London* (London, Cassell, 2000)

Richmond, I.A., *Roman Britain* (Harmondsworth, Penguin, 1955)

Ridley, Jasper, *Elizabeth I* (London, Constable, 1987)

Sala, G.A., *Twice Around the Clock: Or, The Hours of the Day and Night in London* (London, Unknown, 1859)

Sandbrook, Dominic, *Never Had It So Good: A History of Britain from Suez to the Beatles* (London, Little, Brown, 2005)

Savage, John, *England's Dreaming: Sex Pistols and Punk Rock* (London: Faber, 1991)

Schama, Simon, *A History of Britain: Volume I: At the Edge of the World? 3000 BC – AD 1603* (London, BBC, 2000)

Shapiro, James, *1599: A Year in the Life of William Shakespeare* (London, Faber, 2005)

Sinclair, Iain, *Lights Out for the Territory:* (London, Granta, 1997)

Sinclair, Iain, *Sorry Meniscus: Excursions to the Millennium Dome* (London, Profile, 1999)

Sinclair, Iain, *London Orbital* (London, Viking, 2002)

Sinclair, Iain (ed), *London: City of Disappearances* (London, Penguin, 2006)

Sinclair, Iain, *Hackney: That Rose-Red Empire* (London, Hamish Hamilton, 2009)

Sissons, Michael, and French, Philip, *Age of Austerity, 1945-51* (Harmondsworth, Penguin, 1964)

Sitwell, Edith, *The Queens and the Hive* (London, Macmillan, 1962)

Smiley, Jane, *Charles Dickens* (London, Weidenfeld & Nicolson, 2002)

Stenton, Doris Mary, *English Society in the Early Middle Ages 1066-1307* (Harmondsworth, Penguin, 1951)

Southey, Robert, *The Life of Nelson* (London, Grange Books, 2004 re-issue)

Strachey, Lytton, *Eminent Victorians* (London, Chatto & Windus, 1918)

Strachey, Lytton, *Elizabeth and Essex* (London, Chatto & Windus, 1928)

Thomas, Keith, *Religion and the Decline of Magic* (London, Weidenfeld & Nicolson, 1971)

Thompson, E.P, *The Making of the English Working Classes* (London, Gollancz, 1963)

Thomson, David, *England in the Nineteenth Century* (Harmondsworth, Penguin, 1950)

Thomson, David, *England in the Twentieth Century* (Harmondsworth, Penguin, 1965)

Trevelyan, *Ilustrated English Social History: 1* (Harmondsworth, Penguin, 1964)

   Illustrated English Social History: 2 (Harmondsworth, Penguin, 1964)
   Illustrated English Social History: 3 (Harmondsworth, Penguin, 1964)
   Illustrated English Social History: 4 (Harmondsworth, Penguin, 1964)

White, T.H. *The Age of Scandal: An Excursion Through a Minor Period* (London, Cape, 1950)

Whitelock, Dorothy, *The Beginnings of English Society* (Harmondsworth, Penguin, 1952)

Wills, John E., *1688: A Global History* (London, Granta, 2001)

Wright, Patrick, *The River: The Thames in Our Time* (London, BBC, 1999)

Ziegler, Philip, *London at War* (London, Pimlico, 2002)

ADDITIONAL READING:

FICTION

British novelists have been writing about London ever since novels began to be written in the nation: Defoe, Fielding, Thackeray's *Vanity Fair*... Not many people would argue, though, with the claim that Charles Dickens is the greatest novelist ever to make London his main setting. Almost all of his books evoke, dissect, celebrate and damn the city with incomparable genius. *Great Expectations* is my personal favourite, closely followed by *Bleak House, Our Mutual Friend* and *Little Dorrit*. If you have not read any of these, a treat awaits you.

In the last couple of decades, the two British novelists who have concentrated most intensely on London have been Peter Ackroyd (who has also written biographies of various famous Londoners–Dickens, Blake, Sir Thomas More, Chaucer, Turner...) and Iain Sinclair, whose long poem about the deeper mysteries of the town, *Lud Heat*, was the inspiration for Ackroyd's best-selling novel *Hawksmoor*, a Gothic thriller loosely based on the life and buildings of the seventeenth century architect Nicholas Hawksmoor. Ackroyd's other London-based novels include *The Great Fire of London, The House of Dr Dee* (inspired by Queen Elizabeth I's court magician, John Dee) and *Dan Leno and the Limehouse Golem*. Sinclair's novels include his fantasia on a Jack the Ripper theme, *White Chappel, Scarlet Tracings* and *Downriver*. A third writer in much the same vein as Ackroyd and Sinclair is the prolific Michael Moorcock: *Mother London* is the title to pick.

Some other novels of the last century or so which have added to the London saga include (in alphabetical order):

Monica Ali, *Brick Lane*
Martin Amis, *Success, Money, London Fields*
Julian Barnes, *Metroland*
Samuel Beckett, *Murphy*
Elizabeth Bowen, *The Heat of the Day*
Anthony Burgess, *The Doctor is Sick*
Norman Collins, *London Belongs to Me*
Joseph Conrad, *The Secret Agent*
Helen Fielding, *Bridget Jones's Diary*
George Gissing, *New Grub Street*
Henry Green, *Caught*
Graham Greene, *The End of the Affair*
Patrick Hamilton, *Hangover Square, 20,000 Streets Under the Sky*
Robert Irwin, *Satan Wants Me*
Jerome K Jerome, *Three Men in a Boat*
B.S. Johnson, *Christie Malry's Own Double-Entry*
Hanif Kureishi, *The Buddha of Suburbia*
Colin MacInnes: *Absolute Beginners, City of Spades, Mr Love and Justice*
Ian McEwan, *Saturday*
George Orwell, *Keep the Aspidistra Flying, Nineteen Eighty-Four*
Sukhdev Sandhu, *Night Haunts*
Zadie Smith, *White Teeth*
Neal Stephenson, *The Baroque Cycle*
Bram Stoker, *Dracula*
Virginia Woolf, *Mrs Dalloway*
Evelyn Waugh, *Vile Bodies*

MISCELLANY

First, a handful of poems: "London", by William Blake. "London," by Samuel Johnson (after Juvenal), "Upon Westminster Bridge" by William Wordsworth, "The City of Dreadful Night" by James Thomson, *The Waste Land* by T.S. Eliot.

Except during periods of plague and civil war, London has thrived as a centre of plays and players since the great dramatic flowering under Elizabeth, and many of London's dramatists have chosen their home town as both setting and theme.

Many of Shakespeare's history plays have scenes set in the capital (see the first part of *Henry IV*), and his comedies–even when they purport to be set in "Illyria" (*Twelfth Night*) or "Athens" (*A Midsummer Night's Dream*)–obviously draw on his observations of London life.

Ben Jonson's comedies, such as *Bartholemew Fair*, include vivid and still funny portraits of the town and its wicked ways. In fact, Jonson's give a more plausible account of the place than the witty, well-made but often excessively genteel and tepid dramatic works that were standard West End fare until the great theatrical revolt of the mid-1950s, launched from the Royal Court Theatre in Sloane Square.

Shakespeare and Jonson have never truly been matched by London dramatists of later generations, though obviously there are still great pleasures to be had in the likes of Wilde (*The Importance of Being Earnest*), Shaw (*Pygmalion*), Coward, Rattigan, Tom Stoppard, Howard Brenton, Caryl Churchill, Alan Bennett....

There are thousands and thousands of London memoirs, but the greatest of them all is still widely agreed to be the *Diaries* of Samuel Pepys. It is available in many shorter editions. The greatest biography in English, James Boswell's *Life of Johnson*, is also rich in fascinating glimpses of daily London life, and Boswell's *London Journal* (edited F.A. Pottle, 1950) is wonderfully entertaining.

For an extraordinary glimpse into the Elizabethan criminal underworld, track down the inexpensive Penguin paperback collection *Cony-Catchers and Bawdy Baskets*.

A relatively little-known twentieth-century book, Arthur Machen's *The London Adventure or The Art of Wandering* (1924), is well worth seeking out; and anyone who enjoys tales of Bohemian life should read Julian Maclaren-Ross's *Memoirs of the Forties.*, with its boozy yarns of Soho and Fitzrovia.

Finally, Alan Bennett–originally from Yorkshire, but a long-term resident of Camden –has in recent years become almost as well-loved for his published diaries as for his plays.

IMAGE CREDITS

Page 82: W.P.A. Federal Theatre Presents "Faustus" by Christopher Marlowe
Posters: WPA Posters, Prints and Photographs Division, Library of Congress, LC-USZC2-5591

Page 140: Still from the film *From Hell*, 2001, TM & Copyright © 20th Century Fox Film Corp. All rights reserved. Courtesy of Everett Collection

Page 172: LET IT BE, The Beatles, Paul McCartney, John Lennon, Ringo Starr, George Harrison, 1970. Courtesy of Everett Collection

Page 174: Johnny Rotten, lead singer with the Sex Pistols pop group, 1977
© Mirrorpix/Courtesy Everett Collection

Page 176: Punks near Camden Market, London
Photo © Ester Inbar

Page 180: The Wedding of HRH Prince and Catherine (Kate) Middleton Pictured: The married couple appear on the balcony to wave to fans and share a kiss.
© National News and Pictures.
Photo: Jason Green Photoshot/Everett Collection

Page 212: 8. President Vladimir Putin with British Prime Minister Tony Blair in 2000
Photo © Presidential Press and Information Office in Russia

Page 214:
12-2. Photo © Adrian Pingstone
12-3. Photo © Andreas Praefcke

Page 228:
25. Margaret Thatcher
Photo by White House Photographic Office

Page 251:
7. Photo © Andreas Praefcke
8. Photo © Archibald Tuttle

Page 252:
10. Photo © David Caster
11. Photo © Gary Bembridge

Page 253:
13. Photo © DMS
14. Photo © Green Lane

Page 254:
15. Photo © Michael Pead
16. Photo © Louise Ireland
17. Photo © Paddy Briggs

Page 255:
23. Photo © Oxyman

Page 262:
2. Photo © Fan Yang

Page 265:
9. Photo © Xiquinho Silva

9. Photo © Danny Robinson
10. Victoria Embankment, London; 1926 by Lesser Ury
Page 266: Then & Now: LEADENHALL MARKET
Photo © Martin Addison
13. Photo © Peter Trimming
14. Photo © Christine Matthews

Page 267:
16. Photo © Deror avi
19. The Mansion House in London. Engraving by J Woods after a picture by Hablot Browne and R Garland. Published 1837.
20. Photo © Chris Downer

Page 270:
1. © Florence Nightingale Museum

Page 271:
Sidebar Photo © Paul Farmer

Page 272:
8. Photo © ChrisO

Page 273:
9. Courtesy of Founders Arms

Page 274:
12. 49 Cardinal's Wharf (left)
Photo © Peter Holmes

Page 275:
14. Photo by Sir James

Page 276:
18. Photo © Michael Reeve
20. Photo © Aurelien Guichard

ACKNOWLEDGMENTS

Many thanks to John Baxter for introducing, Akira Chiba for commissioning, the indefatigable Heather Corcoran for editing and Peter Straus for agenting.
All the faults and errors that may lurk in this book are my fault and mine alone, and should not be allowed to damage the considerable reputations of those good friends with whom I have explored the streets, the buildings, the literature and the watering holes of London over the decades: Jo Banham (of the Victoria & Albert Museum), Kate Bassett (*Independent on Sunday*), Peter Blegvad (President of the London Institute of Pataphysics), Alastair Brotchie (Secretary of the LIP), Peter Carpenter, Sir Christopher Frayling (Rector Emeritus of the Royal College of Art), Mark Godowski, Dick Humphreys (Tate Britain), Ian Irvine (*The Independent*), Magnus Irving (LIP), Robert Irwin (LIP) Dr Mary-Louise Jennings, Nick Lezard (*New Statesman*), Kevin Loader, the late Tom Lubbock, Kevin Macdonald, Roger Michell, Deborah Mills, Colin Minchin, Tanya Peixoto, Rainer Sanger, Iain Sinclair (author of *London Orbital*), Tom Sutcliffe, Dr Peter Swaab (University College, London), David Thompson (BBC), Prof. Martin Wallen, Prof. Marina Warner, Lisa Williams.
Without my wife, Claire: *nada*.
And finally, warmest thanks to my dedicatees: Hen, Rog, Haz and Em.

ABOUT MUSEYON

Named after the Museion, the ancient Egyptian institute dedicated to the muses, Museyon Guides is an independent publisher that explores the world through the lens of cultural obsessions. Intended for frequent fliers and armchair travelers alike, our books are expert-curated and carefully researched, offering rich visuals, practical tips and quality information.

MUSEYON'S OTHER TITLES

Pick one up and follow your interests...wherever they might go.
For more information vist www.museyon.com

Publisher: Akira Chiba
Editor-in-Chief: Heather Corcoran
Art Director: Ray Yuen
Cover Design: José Antonio Contreras

Maps & Illustration Design: EPI Design Network, Inc.
Assistant Editors: Cotton Delo, Charlie Fish
Copy Editor: Carrie Funk

ABOUT THE AUTHOR

Kevin Jackson compiled *The Oxford Book of Money*,
wrote *Invisible Forms*, *A Guide to Literary Curiosities*,
a book on the Great Pyramid, a number of books on the
cinema, one on the moose, another on vampires and
yet another on fast food in Britain. He was associate
arts editor of the daily newspaper the *Independent*
and film critic for the *Independent on Sunday*. He is
a lifelong Londoner.